dismantle

A Memoir

ANGIE KIEHNE

ISBN: 978-1-963569-40-7 (hard cover)
        978-1-963569-41-4 (soft cover)

Edited by: Amy Ashby

Warren
publishing

Published by Warren Publishing
Charlotte, NC
www.warrenpublishing.net
Printed in the United States

For my darling daughter
Your unconditional love and boundless joy have been vital to my
healing process. Each time we laugh together,
I see a brighter future. I love you with all my heart.

For my younger sister
You lived this story alongside me.
With your selfless support, I dared to seek a better life.
I am so proud of what you have accomplished
and am grateful to have you in the arena with me.

For my ex-husband
You helped me go further than I ever thought possible.
I will always love you.

For my life partner
You are my muse. My best friend.
The happy ending to my story.

Chapter 1
1992

My mother was hidden from view inside her walk-in closet, selecting an outfit for the dance club. I sat on the bed I shared with my older sister, Karina, just outside the open closet door. Pressing my back against the bare white wall, standard in apartments, I read each article and scrutinized every photograph in the library's latest issue of *Travel & Leisure* magazine.

"Oh, Angie," Mom called out as if remembering an item for a grocery list. "Don't ever use the washcloth hanging on the pipe behind the toilet. Antoine uses that to clean his penis after sex."

"It would never occur to me to touch a rag behind a toilet," I said, grimacing.

Mom emerged from the closet, shoehorned into a little black dress that fell scandalously north of her knee. A cropped gold lamé jacket, decorated with a chaotic pattern that called to mind the ambiguous shapes of a Rorschach inkblot test, fought to steal the spotlight away from her red patent-leather heels.

Still lean and toned from her Seattle bodybuilding competition, Mom's glossy blond hair cascaded luxuriously down her back. I pulled a few strands of my long brown hair through my fingers, wondering why it didn't have the same luster as hers.

"Well, what do you think?" she asked, propping her hands on her hips like a model on the runway. Mom loved compliments.

I shrugged. With her bleached hair and red lipstick, Mom looked like a prostitute. Gone were the denim dresses and sandals, the large glasses and the hairy pits that had characterized her for the first twelve years of my life. She only vaguely resembled the mother I used to know in Vermont.

Extending one foot, Mom swiveled her stiletto as if stubbing out a cigarette. "Know what these are called?" she asked, with a mischievous smile. "They're 'fuck-me pumps.' That's what Gloria told me."

"Oh," I said.

Aunt Gloria, having entertained many suitors herself, had been coaching her younger sister on the dating scene, even seeding my mother's clubwear collection with pieces she had outgrown—such as the tacky gold jacket. Initially, the two of them had gone to dance clubs together, but that trend quickly ceased. I assumed it was because they were each other's stiffest competition, both being vivacious blond-haired women who had proclaimed to me individually that "once you go Black, you never go back."

Mom never lied or concealed her activities. I wished she had, as I didn't want to know what was occurring behind the bedroom door when I was sitting on the other side of the wall in the living room—especially given that we lived in a one-bedroom apartment and her bed was mere feet from mine.

"Your father never wanted me to look pretty," Mom said, sliding gold bangles onto her wrist. "He discouraged me from wearing makeup or getting contacts. He'd even tell me it was okay with him if I got fat."

I didn't see what the problem was. That sounded like the ideal relationship to me.

Mom crossed the hall to the bathroom. The familiar sounds of heels clacking against linoleum tile and a compact snapping open faded to white noise as I reveled in photos of overwater bungalows in Fiji.

My reading was stalled once more when Mom returned. She leaned down to apply her stamp of approval to my cheek, rendered in lipstick. The scent of vanilla musk applied to her wrists and behind her ears conjured images of weeknight dancing at the Red Lion Inn and bottles of Zima knocked back with whoever was buying.

Using the sleeve of my blue flannel shirt, I wiped away the waxy residue left on my cheek.

"Listen for your brother's knock at the front door," Mom said.

"Yup," I said obediently.

Presumably at his friend CJ's apartment, Ryan tended to return home only when he was ready for bed. His best friend was a sweet, pudgy kid who lived in our complex. The eight-year-old boys were nearly inseparable, in part due to CJ having a gaming console with all the latest video games.

Karina, being three years older than me, was generally off the hook for babysitting because she had maintained consistent after-school employment since the age of sixteen, as well as a social life.

"Oh, one more thing," Mom said, pausing in the doorway.

"If Jamal ever comes calling for me when I'm not here, don't answer the door. He was convicted of rape a few years back and did a little time for it," she continued, as though reciting the biography of a stranger. "He says he's innocent, and I believe him, but I still don't want him around when I'm not here."

Chapter 2
1987

With everyone in our family loaded up in the van, I imagined how uncharacteristically still our house must be. I peered at its gray facade through the window, wishing to continue playing with my dolls instead of going to worship. But I knew, even as I buckled myself in on the bench seat next to my younger brother Ben, that once I was at the dining table with my siblings savoring the large hash brown pancake Dad would fry up as soon as we got back home, I would take great satisfaction in having completed my spiritual commitment and getting the rest of the day to play.

"Can we listen to music?" Ben asked as we pulled out of the driveway. His light-brown hair hung limply in a bowl cut, save for a few strands at the top that stood on end as though they'd been rubbed vigorously with a balloon. He wore a pilled moss-green sweater, a hand-me-down from Karina, as was the gray sweatshirt I was wearing.

I raised my eyebrows at Ben, then smirked at my sisters who sat in the back seat before I realized he was serious. Heidi grinned and Karina shook her head at the absurd question.

"You know we don't listen to music on the way to worship," Mom said from the passenger seat, holding three-year-old Ryan on her lap. She ran a palm over my youngest brother's auburn curls, which bounced back into place.

Rays of early morning sunshine streamed in through the windshield. Dad drove in reverent silence. Reaching the ashram a few minutes later, Karina, Heidi, Ben, and I climbed out of the sliding door.

"Dad!" I said. "I want to go with you today."

"The worship hall is for twelve and older, Angie," he said. "You might get bored."

"I can do it, Dad," I said eagerly.

"Are you sure you don't want to go with the other kids?" he asked, gesturing at my younger siblings who were already ambling toward the main school building where children's services were led by a woman from our community.

My eyes followed Ben, kicking at pebbles with his scuffed blue sneakers. Heidi and Ryan trailed behind him. I considered how much I enjoyed the parables Suzanne read to us and the game of dodgeball she usually permitted during the last half hour.

"No, I want to stay with you," I said, grabbing hold of Dad's hand. With my forefinger, I traced the textured design on his silver wedding band. It reminded me of a vine embarking on the seemingly impossible task of growing straight up a brick wall, using its tendrils as anchors.

"Oookaaay," Dad said, stretching out his vowels to indicate skepticism at my ability to sit still for an hour and a half. Dad knew everything, from what I should name my dolls when pretending they were from other countries to how I should retrace my steps to find a lost necklace. But he didn't know how determined I was to be with him.

Mom and Karina had already started down the short dirt road that connected the likewise unpaved parking lot to the worship hall. Dad and I followed, joining a silent parade of other worshippers. Former hippies, like my parents, most wore corduroys and sweaters or jeans and sweatshirts.

The sun followed us, moving like the spotlight at a school play across the green leaves of the maples that bowed over the low stone wall along the side of the road. Clinging to Dad's arm, I hopped over the deep ruts remaining from mud season. Caused by winter's melting snow, the mud had turned the ashram's property into a tire-wrenching quagmire.

A smile spread across my face as I looked ahead toward our destination. Made of wood planks and nestled amongst trees alongside a small pond, the worship hall had the cozy, welcoming appearance of a ski lodge. We entered a foyer, removed our shoes, and picked our way carefully between worshipers seated cross-legged on the floor. Not a noise could be heard save for the faint swish of our socks treading on the cobalt-blue carpet.

The building's inner walls were of the same exposed wood as the exterior. A massive stained-glass window at the front featured a lotus, its petals rendered in pale yellow and orange. Just below it hung a framed photo of our guru, resplendent in his white turban and kurta, smiling with immense love. The building was otherwise devoid of ornamentation.

Mom and Karina took a seat on the carpet at the halfway point, and Dad and I sat just behind them. After pulling her ash-blond hair into a low ponytail and adjusting her glasses, Mom fell still. Karina glanced around and smiled at each friend she spotted. A fresh crew cut had left her blond hair feathered at the sides and spiky on top, so short it didn't even meet the collar of her jean jacket.

I looked up at Dad as he stared straight ahead with perfect posture, already withdrawn from his surroundings. Even in repose, his dark eyebrows remained pinched together, which wrinkled his forehead. I perceived it as his attempt to appear aloof, but it was actually a cover for his shyness.

Like the beach at low tide, his close-cropped brown hair had receded high up his pale forehead, save for the peninsular widow's peak left behind. He had brown eyes, a long, narrow nose ending in almond-shaped nostrils, and a beard the color of a burnt-umber crayon. His breath smelled pleasantly of coffee.

Dad's older brother, Eldon, took a seat nearby. He flashed a kind but restrained smile in our direction. I beamed back, wishing I could dash over to hug him. I wondered where his wife, Arlene, was and whether his son, Alan, was at children's worship with my younger siblings.

Eldon was a more somber version of my father, with a narrower face, graying hair, and wire-rimmed glasses. Rather like Eeyore, the depressed donkey from the Winnie the Pooh stories, Dad and Eldon seemed to have never recovered from the loss of their mother. She had passed away from cancer when they were just teens. His three other brothers didn't seem as affected, but then, I hardly knew them.

I turned my gaze, watching our congregation leader, Randall, as he slowly proceeded to the head of the hall. He was dressed in a long black pea coat over a gray sweater and dark slacks, and his shaggy hair and beard resembled steel wool. After sitting cross-legged, facing us on a raised platform, he opened a book to a saved page.

The opening *bhajan* began, a hymn sung in Hindi in a call-and-answer style, led by a volunteer from where he sat on the carpet. Though everyone in the room was White, they all did their best to achieve proper pronunciation while singing in a different language. I followed the voice and saw that it was Malcolm, the jeweler who had made my parents' wedding bands. Already familiar with the tune from children's services, I joined in when it was the congregation's turn to repeat a line. Given his habit of zealously whistling bhajans at home, I was surprised to see Dad remain silent, apparently too self-conscious to participate.

When the singing concluded, Randall proceeded with reading a publication by our guru based on the concepts of karma and reincarnation. Our guiding principle was that one's relationship with God is a private journey on which we should perform selfless service for those in need while maintaining the temple of the body through chastity and ahimsa, or non-violence. This included abstaining from meat, eggs, alcohol, drugs, and tobacco.

In addition to leading the ashram, Randall was also a teacher at Satmardeva, the kindergarten through twelfth-grade private school located on the same property in Heathburn, Vermont. My siblings and I, being students at the school, knew Randall well. I'd always found his soft, rhythmic speech comforting. He took his time reaching the end of each sentence and read an especially meaningful line twice for emphasis.

Sitting attentively through the service, I wanted Dad to see that I was ready to start attending with him from now on. By the closing bhajan, I wondered whether my younger siblings were enjoying dodgeball at that very moment. Regardless, I was right where I wanted to be, by Dad's side.

After the service concluded, the worshipers departed in silence, their movements slow as though performed underwater. Mom and Dad laced up their matching brown waterproof duck boots. As we stepped back out into the sunshine, I clasped Dad's hand. His fingers, which were calloused enough to handle hot bread pans and strum folk songs on an acoustic guitar, curled gently around mine. Our pace quickened to match Mom and Karina's purposeful gait.

"Why are we hurrying?" I asked.

"We need to get home," Dad said, "to open the store for the Sunday rush."

The air crackled as a line of cars snaked through the dirt parking lot. My younger siblings leaned against the side of the van, waiting. With her pixie cut, large brown eyes, and freckled nose, Heidi's head looked comically small rising out of a bulky beige cable-knit sweater. White rubber Wellingtons covered the bottom half of her red corduroy pants.

I felt a warmth radiating throughout my body as though filled with light. It was the same feeling of contentment I got whenever I slipped into Dad's vacated side of the bed early in the morning. Careful not to disturb Mom so I wouldn't get shushed, I liked to snuggle into Dad's pillow and suck my thumb until I fell back to sleep.

"Dad," I said, looking up at him, "I want to live with you forever. I never want to leave home."

He chuckled.

"Oh, I think you'll change your mind someday."

Chapter 3

The basement in our ranch house served as a bakery at one end, while the storefront occupied the other half. Dad arose at three o'clock in the morning six days a week to bake and was done with his shift by the time Mom opened the door to customers.

After breakfast, I'd linger at the dining table in the kitchen. Built for us by Mom's younger brother Dale, who was a carpenter, the tabletop was formed by two wide slabs of lacquered oak that were joined together. With a photo of our guru inlaid in the middle, it served as a reminder to be thankful to God at mealtime.

I liked to watch Dad inspect loaves from the day's batch. He sliced with great precision using a special bread knife, an exaggeratedly long blade with a blunt end rather than a standard pointed tip. Its evenly spaced serration looked like peaked waves rather than the close, sharp teeth or smooth but razor-sharp blades of other knives. I found it fascinating that Dad had a specialized tool for every kitchen task—in this case, to cut into soft bread without crushing it.

Dad would hold a slice of his bread up to the window over the sink to examine its texture in the morning sunlight. Observing his routine was not just a cherished part of my day; it also made me feel like everything was right in the world. Plus, it meant I got to be the beneficiary of the test loaf. Nothing in the entire world was more delicious than a slice of Dad's potato bread still warm from the oven, served with a pat of butter that would melt into the soft nooks and crannies framed by a flaky golden crust.

I'd chatter at Dad about anything on my mind as he moved on to other tasks. If he wasn't listening attentively to me while he ran an electric sharpener to keep his knives in prime shape, oiled his wooden cutting boards for longevity, or prepared meals for the family, I wasn't any the wiser for it. Having exhausted the topic of the moment, I'd run off to play with my siblings or toys.

I didn't tend to think much about the future, beyond playing with those folded paper fortune tellers young girls create to predict which boys they'll marry and whether they'll become doctors or lawyers. I did, however, anticipate that someday Dad was going to teach me how to bake. I'd already gotten some practice whenever he saved a bit of dough for Ben and me. My brother and I would roll the soft, sticky dough into logs and push chocolate chips into them with our fingertips. We'd grin at each other with pride when Dad returned our finished products from his industrial oven, then scurry off to devour our creations.

Chapter 4

Playtime was put on pause one Saturday afternoon when Mom called a family meeting. My siblings and I, still comfortably dressed in pajamas, congregated in the living room where our mother sat on the yellow floral-patterned couch. Passed on to us from another family in the community, the couch was an eyesore, but it was long enough to conveniently accommodate the five of us kids.

I wasn't sure what a family meeting was. It sounded boring. Hovering near one end of the couch with my back against the wood-paneled wall, I hoped that whatever it was it would be over soon so I could return to playing in my bedroom.

Though nearly twelve years old, I was enamored with paper dolls. Standing at ten inches high and printed wearing only white undergarments, the attractive blond woman and her husband with sideswept brown hair had come with a booklet containing an extensive wardrobe. I had used scissors to meticulously free their outfits from the pages, careful to leave the paper tabs intact around the edges. The dolls were a blank canvas upon which I could ascribe any fashion or lifestyle I desired. It was exciting having so many options. The couple effortlessly transitioned from pilgrims to Victorian high-society types and from rustic outdoor adventurers to modern jet-setters. Each figure was placed on a strategically folded base, enabling them to stand on their own. They had to be handled gingerly, however, or else the individual components came apart.

"I'm thinking about having our family move," Mom announced, wrapping her arms around Heidi and Ryan, who flanked her on the couch. "What do you think of that idea?"

"Where?" Ben asked, wrinkling his nose. Sitting on the floor with one knee up, he pushed a small toy sports car back and forth on the carpet.

"Oh, maybe to North Carolina or Washington state," Mom said, in the same singsong manner I'd heard her recite "This Little Piggy" while playing with Ryan's toes when he was a baby. She was wearing her favorite tie-dyed shirt streaked with turquoise, lavender, and violet, which reminded me of twilight.

"Why would we move to either of those places?" I asked.

"Well, Grandma and Grandpa are in Southern Pines, and Gloria is near Seattle," she said. "So we'd already know someone in both places." She paused to smile at each of us.

I glanced over at Dad, who was sitting stiffly in an armchair. He looked uncomfortable despite wearing jeans and a faded burgundy T-shirt. He remained silent, which wasn't unusual. Whenever we kids asked him if we could spend the night at a friend's house or take a donut from the pastry rack in the bakery, he'd always respond, "Go ask your mother."

"It'll be exciting to live somewhere different, where we can have new adventures," Mom said.

While we had visited my mother's parents in North Carolina several times, we had never been to Seattle before. The most I knew about the area was from a postcard featuring the Space Needle, which Aunt Gloria had sent after relocating from Vermont to the West Coast.

"Which place do you prefer?" asked Karina, perched at the far end of the couch.

"I'm leaning toward Washington," Mom said. "That'll put us close enough to California that we could plan a family trip to Disneyland."

Ben sucked in air, and Heidi squealed with delight.

"Disneyland!" I exclaimed, leaning forward. I'd been envious of friends who'd gotten to vacation at Disney. Our annual summer trip to Maine, where we would stay in rental cottages within walking distance of the ocean, was discontinued by the time Ryan was born because my parents couldn't afford it anymore.

Why does Mom want to move so soon after all the renovations on our house were completed? I wondered. Over the years, central air replaced our wood-burning stove, Grandma gifted us a dryer, which meant Karina and I didn't have to hang the family's wet laundry outside on the clothesline anymore, an extension added two extra bedrooms as our family grew, and last, the exterior of the house took on new life after being transformed from white to Briarwood gray. It was a color choice over which Mom had long deliberated, and we had all agreed, as our family collected in the front yard to admire the results, that it was a warm, welcoming shade that suited our home perfectly.

We had all our needs met in Vermont. My parents got to work out of the house and be their own bosses. The best part about their jobs for us kids was that they were always available. Since Dad's shift finished by the time my siblings and I ate breakfast, he was there to tend to our needs. On nonschool days he took us on excursions during which he taught us to be strong swimmers at the lake, use a carving knife to whittle wood, and how to identify edible wintergreen berries and mushrooms. With a glimmer of excitement in his eyes, Dad would silently point out hawks soaring overhead or deer in the underbrush. When we chased him around the playground calling, "Tag! You're it!" he would whisk himself just out of reach of our fingertips with the uncanny ability of a bullfighter, all the while chortling with gusto. Once, when Karina was attempting to saddle an uncooperative horse, Dad approached the dappled Arabian where it stood and swung himself up onto its back by grabbing hold of the mane. He confidently told my sister that the horse would now accept the saddle. From the pasture fence, my siblings and I stared at each other in open-mouthed wonder at Dad's secret talent, for indeed the horse stood as though rooted to the ground even as it cast furtive glances backward at its unusual rider.

I wondered what Mom could possibly want that life in Heathburn didn't offer. I loved our home, the only one I'd ever known. I loved my school at the ashram, which I'd attended for all six grades and from which I expected to eventually graduate. I had many friends, most of whom I saw both in class and on Sundays at worship.

Sixth grade was drawing to a close for me, and I had been looking forward to a summer spent at the beach and hanging out with my best friend,

Alyssa. She wasn't a fellow student, a member of our community, or even a local. Alyssa had been my best friend since I was six, even though she lived in Massachusetts, roughly two hours away. She and her parents, who were both teachers, spent the better part of the summer at their vacation property a couple of miles up the road from us. We had met when they stopped at our bakery. I was playing outside when a blue-eyed girl with chubby cheeks and sandy-blond curls walked up and asked if she could play with me. Alyssa had no siblings, and her parents were immediately supportive when she found such a close friend in me. We had several playdates that first summer, and as I got older, her parents regularly invited me for sleepovers and to join their family on their annual camping trip.

"I'm okay with going to Washington," Karina told Mom. At fifteen she was mature beyond her years, independent and courageous. It didn't surprise me that she was prepared to charge full speed ahead into the unknown.

Following Karina's lead, I also gave my consent. I trusted my parents' judgment. Surely everything we had in Heathburn would be recreated in our new home, wherever that might be.

Chapter 5

By summer's end, our family was waving goodbye out the back windows of a shuttle bound for Logan Airport in Boston. Uncle Eldon, Aunt Arlene, and my cousin Alan sat on our patio steps watching us drive away. My uncle's shoulders drooped, and his narrow face looked gaunt as he gave a slow, unsmiling wave. In his other hand were the keys, which he was to turn over to the new owners.

Arlene waved stiffly, her dark bouffant hair contrasting with her pale, expressionless face. Alan didn't wave.

"Oh! Eldon is so sad," I said. I broadened my smile and waved more vigorously, hoping to cheer him up. My siblings waved too, calling goodbye even though Eldon couldn't hear us.

As we passed through the security checkpoint at the airport, an agent pulled Mom's purse off the conveyer belt. He fished out the eight-inch-long solid steel shears that had been part of Mom's sewing kit for as long as I could remember.

"Ma'am," he said, "you can't take these aboard the plane."

"They didn't make it into a box in time before we shipped everything," Mom explained. "I promise they'll stay in my bag during the flight." She smiled sweetly.

"We're going to have to confiscate them. They can't go aboard the plane."

"Could I ask you to ship them to me?" Mom suggested.

The agent shook his head. "I'm afraid we don't have the ability to do that, ma'am," he said.

Mom hesitated but had no choice other than to relinquish the scissors so that we could proceed to our gate.

Ben and I, being so close in age, still fed off each other's energy as we had when we were younger. After boarding the TWA plane and taking our seats in a row beside Dad, we explored everything within reach. We opened and closed the window shade, fiddled with various buttons overhead, and accidentally summoned a flight attendant whom Dad waved away with embarrassment. Even when he snapped at us to stop fooling around, it didn't dampen our spirits, especially once compact TV dinners, something we'd never seen before, were delivered to our tray tables.

In the row behind us, Karina was teaching Heidi how to play cat's cradle with a long looped string.

"No, not that one—pick it up from the left side," I heard my older sister say.

"I got it!" Heidi replied.

Up until that point, our family had traveled solely by car, my parents taking turns behind the wheel, keeping their energy up with gas station coffee in order to reach our destination in one straight shot. At the start of a trip, they'd load up our van with luggage, snacks, and a bucket for urine or vomit, and off we'd go to visit Dad's father in Lake Charles, Louisiana, or Mom's parents who had retired in Southern Pines, North Carolina. Once we had even driven to New York to see our guru when he was visiting from India.

On that trip, Mom, who wasn't accustomed to city driving, maneuvered our van anxiously after pulling off the highway into the Bronx. Coming to a halt at a stop sign under a massive metal bridge, she let out a long guttural sigh while scanning left and right. The intersection wasn't governed by a light, and traffic from both directions was heavy. After several minutes of horns rising in volume from behind us, Mom mumbled words it was probably best we couldn't hear as she pressed the gas pedal to the floor. Our van swerved across the intersection to the left, sending all seven of us lurching to the right before snapping up straight again. From the passenger seat, Dad pressed a hand against the dashboard to steady himself. Meanwhile, the frenzy in the back seats reached a feverish pitch.

"We're starving!" we reminded our parents.

"Just wait until we reach the event hall!" Mom said. "There will be sticky buns and oatmeal."

"What's a sticky bun?" I asked.

"Uh, it's like a cinnamon roll," Dad said, rushing his words together while scanning the road ahead for obstacles.

"Sticky buns and oatmeal, sticky buns and oatmeal," Ben and I began chanting, alternately breaking into fits of giggles. For some reason, we found this food combination hilarious. We squirmed on our bench seat and pushed against each other with our shoulders, prevented only by our seat belts from engaging in a good-natured wrestling match.

"You know what you're gonna get?" I asked Ben.

"What?"

"Sticky buns and oatmeal!" I cried.

Our cacophony was cut short when Mom swerved into the event hall's parking lot. Freedom from the car and a nice breakfast were only moments away. I pressed my nose against the side window, searching for any sign of sticky buns.

Having gotten lost so many times along the way, we found that the breakfast buffet had long since been cleaned out by punctual attendees. Mom asked around the lobby if there was any food left but kept being directed back to the same table where only a smattering of crumbs indicated that sustenance had once been there. Just then, she caught the attention of a fellow devotee whom she hadn't seen in years.

"Evelyn!" the man exclaimed. "Every time I see the Kiehnes, your family has grown!" His gaze passed from the toddler in Mom's arms on down the line, each of us wriggling by our mother's side from hunger and the pressing need for a bathroom.

I gave this stranger the stink eye for what felt to me like a judgmental observation, though I harbored an uneasy sense that my parents were out of control. While our faith didn't explicitly discourage the use of contraceptives, my parents behaved as though it did.

Chapter 6

Ever one to make an impression, Gloria met us at the Seattle-Tacoma Airport in a shiny black limo that looked straight out of the movies. I gasped in delight as I approached my aunt, who stood by the back door with a jolly smile.

"Welcome to Washington!" she called out boisterously.

Rather than mask her obesity as some might by wearing dark solids or ruched material, Gloria sported a patchwork-patterned silk jacket in vibrant shades of red, orange, and yellow over a gold-sequined top, turquoise ankle pants, and white tasseled loafers. Standing out boldly from just beneath her short-cropped blond hair, which was styled in moussed waves, was a pair of clip-on pearlescent domes with enormous gold hoops suspended from the bottom. The earrings seemed to have an energy of their own, swinging wildly back and forth every time my aunt turned her head. Her pale, fleshy face was done up with turquoise eye shadow, pink rouge, and fuchsia lipstick.

Gloria worked at the headquarters of a large timeshare company, a job that had relocated her from Vermont to Washington by way of several major cities across the country. Taking full advantage of her employee discount, she vacationed every year in Hawaii, Lake Tahoe, or Las Vegas.

She hugged each of us before we slipped one by one into the car.

"Hello, Bruce!" she said playfully as she embraced my father.

I smirked at the sight of him stiffly suffering the physical contact. He had never been able to mask his disdain for Gloria, but I didn't know why he disapproved of her. Was it her multiple divorces? That she wasn't apologetic about enjoying life to its fullest, eating whatever she liked, dating whomever she pleased, and betting at the racetrack? Or that she had, on occasion, teased my parents about their religion and dietary choices? All I knew was that whenever Mom used to take us to Gloria's lakeside cottage in Vermont, Dad refused to accompany us, and Gloria never came to our house.

As the driver loaded our luggage into the trunk, our cheerful hostess opened a bottle of sparkling cider and handed a plastic flute of the sweet beverage to each of us. I sat back against a plush bench seat. It was difficult to sip the cider when I couldn't stop smiling.

"I can't believe we're actually in a limo," I said to Karina. She grinned back.

"Where's Jason?" Ben asked, referring to our eleven-year-old cousin.

"He had to stay home," Gloria said, "to make sure there was room for everyone in the limo."

"Do you ride around in this all the time?" he asked, with a crooked grin on his face.

"No, silly," she said, chuckling.

"What does this do?" my seven-year-old sister Heidi asked, pressing a button on the wall.

"That opens the window to the driver," Gloria said, her earrings sparkling as they reflected the unearthly glow of the ceiling's blue wrap-around lighting.

Once the divider descended, my aunt used the opportunity to instruct the driver to take the long way home so that we could pass by downtown Seattle. We would be staying with her in Bellevue, just outside the city, until my parents could find a house to rent.

My siblings and I chatted excitedly as Gloria and Mom caught up.

"Look at that!" Ben squealed, pointing out the window.

"We're heading through Seattle now," Gloria said. Everyone turned to look out the windows.

"There's the Space Needle!" I cried. I recognized it from the postcard my aunt had sent us. Like a glowing UFO resting atop a white pedestal, it stood out in the dark amongst the surrounding cluster of office buildings.

To already be engaging in such glamorous activities as taking flights, riding in limos, and drinking pretend champagne seemed to promise great things ahead. Yet even amid all that decadence, an uneasiness began to manifest. My gaze darted from one smiling face to the next, ending with Dad's strained look. The realization that our move was permanent came into sharp focus, and my thoughts shifted to cataloging everything I knew and loved that had been left behind.

When Mom had first broached the subject of moving, the conversation felt as far-fetched as when Ben and I discussed what we'd do with a million dollars: just as I knew the unlikelihood of winning all that money, I hadn't believed this was a realistic scenario either. Yet when Mom raised it again the next day and the day after that, it became clear that though she had extended the courtesy of making us feel we were part of the decision-making process, it wasn't a hypothetical scenario at all. The decision had, in fact, already been made.

I hadn't realized that a cross-country move meant parting with so many beloved possessions, like Dad's vinyl collection and the vintage record player cabinet I would have liked to inherit someday. Most of our belongings were distributed to relatives and other members of the community, as my parents couldn't afford to ship the entire contents of our house. A classmate's younger sister was the lucky beneficiary of my precious canopy bed. I had felt a pang of jealousy to watch the dismantled frame leave my room. A few years earlier, I had returned home from a playdate to find the captivating white bed with its glorious unicorn-and-rainbow lavender comforter and matching ruffled canopy—a surprise gift from my parents. Now the bed was gone before I had even gotten the chance to outgrow it.

As the Seattle skyscrapers were swallowed up by the silent blackness behind us, the discomfort of an unknown fate left me feeling like a cat crouched inside a carrier destined for the veterinary clinic. In less than twenty-four hours, our lives had completely and irrevocably changed. After all, we hailed from a town so rural it had been named for the first family to settle there, and we never passed a single stoplight when we hauled our garbage to the dump. There was no home to go back to now. Suddenly, I wasn't sure whether I might laugh or cry.

Chapter 7

After a few weeks at Gloria's house, where my parents occupied the guest room and we kids slept on the living room floor using a mixture of sleeping bags and blankets, we moved into a rambler on the easternmost side of Bellevue.

The house was indistinguishable from all the rest in the neighborhood, except for its red exterior, while most others had pastel or neutral tones. Each was set on a narrow lot with a short driveway, a carport, and a fenced backyard.

Mom and Dad took the largest bedroom off the short end of the L-shaped house, while at the long end, Heidi got the smallest room, the boys slept in bunk beds in another, and Karina and I shared a full-size bed in the fourth room.

At the end of our street was a recreation center with a swimming pool, where, to our delight, Mom signed us up for a family membership. In addition to the privilege of swimming anytime we wanted, Ben and I also started taking a karate class there.

Mom and Dad still took turns cooking dinner for us; only now when it was Mom's turn, she sang along to the raspy, impassioned tunes of Melissa Etheridge. She was in her own world when she listened to the tape. Neither of my parents had been in the habit of listening to music at home before, although Dad occasionally played folk songs on his acoustic guitar for his own enjoyment.

We no longer officially practiced our faith as no one of our religion lived in Bellevue as far as my parents were aware, and thus there was no means for us to observe our former Sunday practices.

Dad listened to tapes of recorded Sunday services in private. For Mom, our spiritual guru had been replaced with secular ones as she amassed self-help books. I didn't understand where this new fixation came from. Everything had been perfect in Vermont; why was help suddenly needed?

Chapter 8

Dad found that bakeries in the region only paid minimum wage, which told me they didn't appropriately value the skills of accomplished bakers. Not one of the shops where he inquired recognized his God-given talent or celebrated the fact that he had established his own bakery.

Since baking evidently would no longer pay the bills, Dad cast his net wider. He wasn't about to start wearing a suit though. Neither ties nor cufflinks had ever once been presented to him on Father's Day. The fact that Dad tucked his denim button-up shirt into his jeans on his wedding day, as I'd seen in a photo, was his way of acknowledging the formality of the occasion.

His sole concession now was to shave off his beard, though he did leave a mustache. It was my first time seeing his chin. My siblings and I protested the new look, although there was nothing to be done about it after the fact. Dad chuckled at our reaction, but I sensed he wasn't pleased about having to shave either. I wondered whether the facial hair had been hurting his chances of being hired, for whereas beards were commonplace in rural Vermont, not a single man in Bellevue sported one.

Over the first few months, Dad dropped fifteen pounds, which he attributed to not eating at his own bakery anymore. He had always been relatively fit, with muscular arms and a broad chest that he didn't have to do anything to maintain outside of his physically demanding work. Given that what was left of his hair was fading to gray, the combined effect of the weight loss left him starkly gaunt.

Eventually, Dad accepted an unlikely role as a teaching assistant at a Montessori school. He purchased an orange Volkswagen van to accommodate our large family. My siblings and I were embarrassed to be seen in it because there were no other holdovers from the seventies on the road in Bellevue. Worst of all, the van occasionally refused to start. Whenever the engine sputtered out, Dad had to push the vehicle from the open driver's side door. My siblings and I would duck down on the black perforated-vinyl seats, which grew unbearably hot and sticky in the sun. Only after hearing Dad jump in behind the wheel as the engine sprung to life would we lift our heads.

Mom found employment as an administrative assistant at Eddie Bauer headquarters and secured financing to acquire a two-door Ford Festiva hatchback for commuting. Next, she put a Sears credit account to use building a new wardrobe since she owned nothing that would qualify as business casual.

Regularly engaging in home workouts, Mom used a television set, purchased expressly for playing aerobics videos, and a large mirror propped against the living room wall.

Whereas since her teens she had kept her straight hair parted down the middle and tucked behind her ears, she now used a blow dryer on her newly sheered bangs to create voluminous layers. She applied foundation and mascara before going to work. It was my first time seeing her with makeup on.

While Dad's weight loss was unintentional and he did away with his beard simply to fit in, Mom exuded pride and confidence after each upgrade to her appearance and wardrobe. After the final step of trading in her glasses for contacts, Mom was the very image of a modern woman.

Chapter 9

On weekends, Karina returned home late from her shift at the movie theater in the local mall, marked with the telltale scent of buttered popcorn.

Already six feet tall, she towered over my siblings and me. I found it interesting that although she was closer to Mom, she had inherited Dad's height and his long, narrow face and nose. She, like the rest of us, shared our father's brown eyes, rather than Mom's blue-green hue.

Karina was a lean tomboy who still kept her sandy-blond hair close-cropped, though it had grown out enough to no longer be considered a crew cut. Sitting at the edge of our bed in the dark, she'd pull off her white tube socks and use one like dental floss to clean between each toe. Then she'd toss the socks into the nearby hamper and recline onto her pillow, at which point I would bury my nose in her hair and inhale deeply.

"Go to sleep, Ang!" she would whisper, gently pushing me away. Even in the dark, I could tell she was smiling though.

"Your hair smells so good!" I would say, continuing sharp inhalations for comedic effect. "Did you sit inside the popcorn machine?"

"You're ridiculous," she would say, chuckling.

With the scent of popcorn lingering in the air even as I rolled over to my side of the bed, it conjured up images of the glorious Crossroads multiplex. The most exciting venue I had ever laid eyes on, its grand entry was accentuated by a glass steeple and neon lights above the box office.

The bright facade welcomed passersby inside the massive lobby, which had a concession stand on either side. Even with the lobby's vaulted ceiling, the alluring scent of hot butter permeated the area as the lively sound of popcorn popping reverberated throughout. The individual theaters featured comfortable chairs on a tiered floor, the likes of which I had never before seen.

Back in Heathburn we'd take a twenty-minute drive to the nearest theater, and it only featured a single film at a time. When I watched *Back to the Future* there in 1985, the venue—which was squeezed in amongst mom-and-pop shops across from the public library—was already over a decade old. Thus, I assumed all theaters had dingy marquees with missing letters and rows of rickety seats on a flat floor, making it difficult to see over the head of the person in front of you.

Now that Karina worked at a theater, we had access to free tickets, and my siblings and I were only too happy to take advantage of this perk. Armed with a bucket of popcorn and a package of Twizzlers, I could easily enjoy two movies in a row while keeping an eye out for a third option. I watched the thriller *Tremors*, the Christmas comedy *Home Alone*, and the fantastical *Edward Scissorhands* multiple times. Karina even snuck me into the R-rated film *Pretty Woman*. On a really good day, we also got to have masala dosas for dinner from Bite of India in the mall's food court.

Chapter 10

While we had been accustomed to taking the bus to school each day in Vermont, now my younger siblings and I would walk there and back together, since the elementary and middle schools were next door to each other and less than a mile from our house.

On the first day of classes, I donned my best outfit: a pair of beige linen slacks and a long-sleeved turquoise top with ruffles around the collar and hem.

My school was a sprawling single-story structure comprised of long hallways lined with lockers and squeaky linoleum floors. Having never seen lockers in person nor used them before, I continued to use my backpack to carry whatever I needed for the day. I was issued a printed class schedule that outlined which room number I should report to and when, along with each teacher's surname. Given that at Satmardeva students had been on a first-name basis with staff, it felt oddly distant to address my teachers by "Mr." or "Ms."

It was also a foreign concept to keep my shoes on when I arrived on campus instead of leaving them in the foyer to help maintain clean floors. We were to pledge allegiance to the flag before the first class got underway, and while my peers recited it word for word, I moved my lips silently so as not to let on that I wasn't familiar with it. Having lunch in a cafeteria was just like I'd seen in the movies, though I brought sandwiches from home since Mom and Dad couldn't afford school lunches for five children. We were unaware of the federally assisted meal program that would qualify us for low-cost or even free lunch, and the cafeteria didn't have much we could eat anyway.

Not meeting any other vegetarians made me acutely aware of how little I had in common with my peers. Ben told me that his dietary restrictions were mocked by other boys at school. On one occasion, my entire class participated in a discussion about the novelty of having a vegetarian in their midst, with questions spurred by the teacher himself. I resolved not to tell anyone anything more about our differentness unless I absolutely had to, like when a friend's mother offered me a ham sandwich as a polite hostess would do.

A Mormon friend spoke confidently about not watching R-rated films, and a Jehovah's Witness friend displayed no signs of self-consciousness when announcing to the teacher that she would wait in the hall while the class watched a Christmas movie. But no one had a guru, and I revealed nothing about my beliefs to anyone, not even my friends.

The trouble was, my siblings and I were not only raised differently but also lacked the tools to cope outside a community of like-minded individuals. For the first twelve years of my life, being a vegetarian who followed a guru's teachings had been no more unusual in my eyes than being a left-handed girl who had a sweet tooth and whose favorite color was purple. I'd never had to explain my beliefs or diet to anyone in Heathburn because, there, these weren't differentiating factors. By leaving the confines of the community, however, these core defining attributes made us perpetual outsiders.

I felt I would have more in common with the Indian boy in my class than the tall White girl who wore turquoise eyeshadow and had three piercings in each ear. I wanted to ask the boy if he had ever heard of my guru, but I was too shy to initiate the conversation. If he hadn't, it would require an explanation from me that I wasn't prepared to give in public.

It turned out that Star, the girl who wore makeup, was a nice person. She looked older than everyone else, but perhaps that was due to her height and seriousness. She talked to me about unfamiliar things like leasing a horse, while leaning against the window ledge. With her limp blond hair, jeans, and sweatshirts, she looked like she didn't care what anyone thought about her. She had an air of confidence I both envied and felt drawn to.

Chapter 11

That first winter we saw only one inch of snow.

"Are you kidding me? School was canceled for this?" Karina said as my siblings and I stood looking at the backyard through sliding glass doors.

In Vermont when twelve inches of dense snow appeared in our yard overnight, and we fully expected to stay home, we were routinely dismayed to find that plows had already cleared the roads and school was still in session.

Despite the minimal accumulation, Ryan couldn't wait to play in it anyway. He donned a blue one-piece snowsuit and headed outside. We watched him scrape at the shallow, slushy snow with his mittens.

"Poor kid. That's so sad," Karina said, shaking her head.

"Yeah, that's not even real snow," I said. "Remember when Dad used to make us hot chocolate?"

"Yeah!" said Ben, looking over at me with a grin.

Heidi pressed her forehead against the door. "Yeah," she repeated.

When school was canceled after an overnight storm, my siblings and I would play on the snow-covered lawn until our dampened snowsuits clung heavily to our chilled limbs. Only then would we retreat into the warmth of the house to change into pajamas and congregate in the kitchen where Dad could be counted on to have a pot of hot chocolate simmering on the stove for us. It was made with real melted chocolate whisked into fresh-brewed coffee and warmed milk.

Mom would chide Dad for serving coffee to us, the only grown-up beverage they enjoyed since they didn't partake in alcohol.

"They like it," he would say, with a twinkle in his eye.

Though there was snow on the ground now, there was no pot of hot chocolate simmering on the stove. Both Mom and Dad were at work. They didn't have as much time or energy to keep up old traditions since they no longer worked out of the house.

My siblings eventually lost interest and moved on to other activities while I lingered at the door. Watching Ryan twist a small snowball on top of a slightly larger one to create a malnourished snowman, my mind drifted back to a typical winter morning in Vermont.

Awakening to the whooshing sound of the central heating unit kicking on, I'd gaze out the window opposite my canopy bed at the picturesque snow-laden trees in our backyard, then leap from the covers to crouch over the narrow grate alongside the wall. The warm rush of air would send my nightgown ballooning out around me, like Cinderella twirling at the ball. The enticing scent of baking bread would envelop me.

"Hello, Dad!" I'd call through the metal slats of the grate, then race downstairs to the bakery. Loitering next to the automatic dough mixer, which stood at my height, I'd marvel as Dad would gently drop doughnut batter into the fryer and pull tray after tray of perfectly formed baguettes from the industrial oven.

Chapter 12

As Ben, Heidi, and I returned home from school one afternoon, we stopped short at the curb. Dad was standing on the front lawn with a little girl we'd never seen before.

"Who's this?" I asked.

Dad crouched down next to the girl, who looked to be about five, and beamed at her. She clasped her hands and smiled at us shyly.

"Liliana," Dad addressed the girl, "these are my kids, Angie, Ben, and Heidi."

I didn't look around to assess whether my siblings were smiling politely or not, for I couldn't take my eyes off the unexpected visitor. She had brown eyes and long brown hair with short-sheared bangs—nearly the spitting image of myself when I was her age. I felt displeased by her presence, perturbed that she got to spend time with my father while I was in class.

"Liliana is from the Montessori school," Dad said to us as he rose to his feet. "I'm going to be providing after-school care for her on weekdays."

"Here?" I asked.

"Yes," he said.

"Why?"

"To pick up extra income," he said.

I turned and went into the house. Ben followed me, likely out of disinterest for the newcomer, while Heidi remained outside with Dad and the little girl.

Chapter 13

The cost of living in Bellevue far exceeded that of Heathburn. When my parents' financial reserves dwindled, cost-cutting measures became imperative. The first thing on the chopping block was the recreation center membership, which meant no more swimming or karate. It felt worse to have had the benefit and lost it than to have never known it was an option in the first place.

On weekends Dad drove up into the hills, where every house was a mansion, to do yard work for his colleague Maude and her husband. They needed help maintaining their large property, and it was another way for Dad to earn money off the books.

❧

While I had never given much thought to the appearance of my severely crooked teeth before, I noticed that every student at school seemed to either have braces or already had them and now sported straightened teeth. My two front teeth on top smashed inward, while the lower set overlapped, and the smaller ones that flanked them angled in the opposite direction, like the folds of an accordion. I became self-conscious after realizing their condition revealed our poverty to others, and for the first time in my life, I saw a stark distinction between the haves and the have-nots. It was painfully clear which category my family fell into. Back in our hometown, most members of the community were of a similar socioeconomic status, and I was therefore blissfully unaware of how my parents barely scraped by.

"We can't afford braces," Mom said when I asked her to take me to the orthodontist. "We're still paying off debt to your dentist in Vermont from all the fillings you kids got over the years."

Not knowing anything about health insurance, I wondered how wealthy the other students' parents had to have been to afford braces.

To earn a little spending money, Ben and I shared a paper route on alternating weekends. When it was my turn to deliver, I borrowed his bike. A booth just up the street provided me with a large canvas sack filled with papers, which I'd hang from the handlebars.

There were always a few extra copies after completing the delivery to subscribers, so I'd bring one home for Mom. Not for the news, which my parents didn't follow, but for the rentals page. Mom continually scanned the ads looking for lower-rent houses in the area.

When Mom located one such possibility just a few blocks away, the whole family went to tour it. My siblings and I frenetically explored the large house while my parents remained with the broker discussing the finer details. As we dashed in and out of each bedroom on the second floor, one of us would holler, "I call this room!"

We all agreed we loved the house. Mom set about writing a heartfelt letter to the owners telling them what a good family we were. She proudly read it aloud to us, closing with: "We will care for this house like it was our own and, with a little elbow grease and TLC, leave it in even better condition for the next tenants."

My whole family was certain this was going to be our next home, both because we wanted it so badly and because Mom's letter seemed sufficiently moving. However, she never heard back from the owners. A couple of weeks later when we drove past the house, we noticed that the rental sign was no longer in the front yard.

"I thought for sure my letter would work," Mom said, her face hanging with disappointment as she sat at the table, a fresh rentals page in hand. I felt sad that her efforts hadn't paid off.

Even after my parents trimmed expenses in every way possible and borrowed Karina's savings of a few hundred dollars, they found it still wasn't enough to stay afloat. We had no other choice than to return to Gloria's house. Not to her main floor, as she now had an exchange student occupying the guest room, but to the basement.

As we prepared to move, Mom said I would have to give up the bunny I had recently adopted from my science teacher when the classroom pet gave birth to a litter.

"It's just not going to work," she told me while packing a box. "You need to get rid of her."

I had built a cage for Minna myself out of chicken wire. I worked on it after school each day with my teacher's guidance until it was complete and I could bring my new pet home.

As disappointed as I was to give Minna up, I understood that a dark basement was no place for a bunny. I arranged to give her to one of Heidi's friends, taking comfort in the knowledge that, given the circumstances, she would have a better life where she was going.

Chapter 14

On moving day my parents did most of the heavy lifting—and most of the frowning. Whereas the first time we'd stayed with her, Gloria had given my parents her guest room and we kids slept in the living room using a variety of sleeping bags and blankets, now she was putting us all in the basement.

An entrance off the back patio led straight down to the basement. Both Mom and Dad wore stone faces as they held up either end of the large, unframed mirror my mother had been using in the rental for her home workouts. After deliberating over angles, Mom started down the short staircase first.

My siblings and I clustered along the railing at the top to watch as my parents strained to hold the glass upright. Suddenly the bottom corner caught on the last of the concrete steps, sending shock waves rippling through the mirror and shattering it. Huge shards cascaded around Mom's feet with a terrible clanging that reverberated against the cement wall.

My siblings and I looked at each other in disbelief. The frown on Mom's face deepened as she surveyed the mess, and she let out a long guttural sigh. It struck me that she seemed more deflated than necessary over a broken mirror; after all, it could be replaced.

The only furniture we still had from Vermont was our yellow floral-patterned couch, a loveseat, and our treasured dining table. Once those and the rest of our belongings were moved in, Gloria generously welcomed us to help ourselves to snacks in her kitchen, which opened out onto the slate-tiled patio. With cookies in hand, my siblings and I gathered around my cousin Jason in the backyard to marvel at his Nintendo Game Boy.

Jason had spiky chestnut hair, blue eyes, and a wide nose. He already stood at my height, though a year younger than me, and his black Depeche Mode T-shirt hung loosely on his bony frame.

Over Jason's shoulder, I noticed that Mom had silently appeared on the patio and was resting in a lounge chair. She wasn't reclining with her feet up, however. Rather, she sat off to one side of the chair with her shoulders slumped forward. Her face was drawn as she stared without blinking into the distance, seeming not to take notice of the blooming rhododendrons that lined the yard nor the songbirds chirping from nearby trees.

I couldn't understand why my mother stared as blankly as the subjects of Depression-era portraits. At least we weren't homeless or starving, and we still had each other. Even as I moved into position to snap a photo of her with the plastic wind-up camera I'd received for my last birthday, Mom paid me no mind. Working the thumb and forefinger of both hands, she picked at the uneven dry skin around her nails. Always, while in repose, her fingers kept as busy as a ghost crab sifting through sand for food.

Chapter 15

Mom and Dad kept us enrolled at our same schools with the reasoning that we'd return to the east side eventually. This required a long drive back across town early enough to deliver each of us to our respective destinations on time. With everyone getting ready simultaneously each morning and only one bathroom hardly bigger than a closet, we had no choice but to embrace an open-door policy. There was often a child on the toilet, another in the shower stall, and a third brushing his or her teeth at the sink.

Though we were living in such close quarters, I never saw Dad less than fully dressed and ready to be productive. Both modest and an extraordinarily early riser, he was not one to lounge about in a bathrobe or be caught in his underwear. Mom, on the other hand, had never been bashful about crossing from the shower to her bedroom nude, so perhaps the lack of privacy was not as much of an adjustment for her.

Once, back in Vermont, my cousin Alan had come over to play with Ben and me. Mom exited the bathroom fresh from a shower. While her hair was wrapped up in a towel, everything south—including her untamed bush—was exposed to the light of day. My cousin stood motionless, blushing all the way up to his hairline.

"Oh—hi, Alan," Mom had said, unabashedly, as she turned the corner toward her bedroom.

Ben and I broke into a fit of giggles at the look of terror on Alan's face as he fled without so much as a word. It was comical picturing him scurrying home to tell Uncle Eldon and Aunt Arlene. Then again, being as odd as he was and so young, he likely wasn't capable of describing such a scene to his parents.

While there was fortunately wall-to-wall carpeting in the basement rather than a standard cement floor, the beige frieze was stained in several areas where my aunt's Persian cat had relieved himself. The faint odor of urine still lingered.

As there were no dividing walls save for the one formed by the central staircase leading up to the main floor of the house, my parents hung sheets from the ceiling to create the illusion of three bedrooms: one for themselves, one for my sisters, and one for my brothers, all of whom shared beds. I used a walk-in closet for a bedroom, with a mauve one-armed chaise wedged inside for a bed. My possessions and clothes were stored in the built-in cubbies that lined the opposite wall.

"I got the best room!" I announced when Karina peeked her head in through the doorway with her eyebrows raised.

"Your bed doesn't look very comfortable though," she said, nodding at the chaise.

"I think it'll be fine," I said. I wasn't worried since it was only a temporary living arrangement.

Chapter 16

While we had the convenience of a full-sized refrigerator, the only cooking appliances were a two-burner hot plate and a microwave. I wondered if my father felt lost without an oven. A washer and dryer competed for space in the same area, and sharing it with Gloria meant that every time she needed to do laundry, she was in our kitchen.

With my parents still living paycheck to paycheck, Dad began accompanying my aunt to Costco once a month to stock up on supplies in bulk. Even though we lived just beneath Gloria, Dad still did everything in his power to avoid interacting with her, and being forced to rely on her for help must have chapped his hide. He would return from their shopping excursions with cases of macaroni and cheese, frozen peas, and economy tubs of margarine, unsweetened peanut butter that had to have the oil pooled at the top of the jar stirred into it, and eerily dark strawberry preserves.

Back in Vermont, our fridge had been stocked with gourmet products, like chèvre, dijon mustard, and homemade mayonnaise (made by Dad without eggs, of course). We dined on savory zucchini pie, corn chowder, and Indian fare such as homemade chai and lentil dal. And we only ever ate bread fresh from the oven. We now had to settle for comically long loaves of spongy whole wheat bread. Powdered whey whisked into cold tap water replaced fresh milk after Dad observed that we wantonly consumed too much of the real thing, which had soared in price upward of two dollars and fifty cents a gallon.

"This tastes like chalk water!" I exclaimed upon sampling the new concoction.

"Well," Dad responded curtly, "you don't have to drink it if you don't like it."

By reclaiming the dimes I kept tucked into the front tab of my black penny loafers, combined with change borrowed from friends, I could purchase chocolate milk from the school cafeteria.

I took up babysitting a five-year-old boy across the street as much for the benefit of sandwiches made with smooth, sugar-laden peanut butter spread on fluffy white bread as for the spending money. The fact that the boy refused to eat anything other than a peanut butter sandwich for lunch was a great selling point: each one I prepared for him meant one for me as well, since his mother had given me permission to eat anything in their kitchen.

"Maybe this summer we can go to Disneyland!" I suggested over dinner one evening.

"I don't think that's going to happen this year," Mom said.

Chapter 17

While other girls my age were becoming interested in boys, I was still playing with Heidi as if I were eight years old too. One of our favorite pastimes was playing dress-up.

Ascending the basement staircase and knocking at the closed door would summon Gloria, whom I would politely ask to loan me clothing for this purpose. Leading me to the second of her overstuffed closets, the one containing the wardrobe she could no longer fit into, she would hand me several items she had worn as a young model. With the clothing carefully draped over my forearm and a pair of high heels in hand, I would rush back downstairs to examine my score with Heidi. It was exciting to behold the vintage fashion pieces I had seen Gloria wearing in her modeling photos: sleeveless polyester sheath dresses, cropped brocade jackets with three-quarter sleeves, and open-toed heels.

Given that my sister was far too small for any of the clothing, our version of make-believe consisted of me alone getting dressed up and traipsing amongst the wood-paneled walls and hanging sheets like a high-society lady from the nineteen sixties.

When I wasn't playing dress-up, I wore boxy off-brand jeans and T-shirts adorned with cat images. Having noticed that the popular girls at school wore form-fitting Guess jeans, I asked for a pair when Mom belatedly took us back-to-school shopping at Sears.

"We don't have money for brand names," she said, holding up a pair of boxy jeans. "You can get these."

Though I envied the popular girls in their trendy clothes, I was still getting my hair trimmed the same way Mom had always instructed the stylist since my very first haircut: a straight sheering of my bangs just above the brow line, cropped at a ninety-degree angle over the ear, and shoulder-length in back. I didn't wear makeup or even consider doing so.

While doing laps around the school's perimeter for gym class alongside two friends, Louisa surprised me by playfully running her forefinger between my shoulder blades with the intent of snapping my bra strap. The fact that I didn't yet wear one threatened to be exposed.

"Where's your bra?" Louisa blurted far too loudly.

"Oh!" I said, scrambling to produce a reasonable answer while looking around to make sure no one else was in earshot. "I forgot to wear one today!"

Louisa looked at me, eyebrows raised, and burst into laughter. She exchanged a glance with Mimi as though she didn't believe me, or worse, they'd been debating about my undergarment status.

"I don't understand how you could forget to wear a bra," she said, wheezing as we plodded ahead.

"Yeah," I said, forcing a chuckle, "isn't that funny?"

That evening I asked Karina what I should do. She shrugged and briefly stopped chewing her nails.

"Get a training bra," she said, like it was the most obvious answer in the world.

I found Mom and sheepishly informed her that it was time I got a bra. Later, at Sears, every style I tried was scratchy and constricting, as unnatural as I imagined corsets must have felt for Victorian ladies. I loathed shopping for an item I felt obligated to acquire but didn't want. I had been doing a perfectly good job of ignoring the indicators of puberty up until that point, and the fact that wearing a bra hadn't organically crossed my mind meant I probably didn't need one yet. Simply because Louisa might try to snap my bra strap again in the future, I was doomed to suffer stiff white lace chafing against my sensitive skin.

Chapter 18

Eventually, we were able to rent our own house again, this time in the Eastgate neighborhood of South Bellevue. It was a split-level with two bathrooms that afforded our family a decent amount of space in a good neighborhood within walking distance of each of our schools. The manicured lawn was flat enough to pitch a tent for summer sleepover parties, and there was a lovely cherry tree by the back fence.

Dad took a second job as a janitor at a large real estate office. To help keep household expenses down, he started bringing home stacks of stiff, rectangular paper towels that couldn't fit when he restocked the holders on the restroom walls, and partial rolls of toilet paper as he was to replace any that were more than half depleted in the stalls.

After dinner each day, when Dad prepared for his graveyard shift, Mom would plead with him not to leave. From the hallway I'd spy on them, watching as Dad stood just inside the front door with a creased forehead. Mom would clutch at his arm, softly encouraging him to call in sick. It pained me how hard my poor father was having to work and how it left Mom suffering his absence five nights a week.

One evening after Dad departed, I lay on my side across the foot of my parents' bed, propping my head up with one arm. It was uncharacteristic for me to hang out with Mom, but I thought the silly antics of my new teddy bear hamster, Gus, might cheer her up.

Dressed in jeans and a mauve sweatshirt, Mom sat hunched forward at the head of the bed, punching numbers into a calculator. Gus ambled amongst the stacks of bills and receipts surrounding my mother's crossed legs, stopping to sniff the paper. When he began to chew on the corner of an envelope, I leaned forward and nudged him gently with my hand. He returned to exploring the flat landscape of the comforter. Mom sighed, scratched her forehead, and continued her task as though unaware she had company.

"Hey, maybe we can finally go to Disneyland this summer," I said.

"I don't think that's going to be feasible, Angie," Mom said, without looking up from the calculator.

I put Gus back in his cage and joined Karina on her bed. We lay side by side on our bellies, with our heels up in the air, looking at a poster she had taped onto the back of her door. It featured a muscular man with an exposed chest. He had blond, side-swept blond hair and black sunglasses, and his thumbs were hitched through the belt loops of his low-slung jeans.

"Man, he's got a hot bod," my sister said.

I nodded. To have any hope of being a cool teenager like her, it seemed important to follow Karina's cue. Secretly, I didn't know what I would do with a man like that; I wasn't even interested in dating yet.

"Mom and Dad will eventually get their finances back on track, and everything will get better, right?" I asked.

"Yeah, I'm sure it will," Karina said out one side of her mouth as she chewed on a fingernail.

Chapter 19

While Heathburn had lacked diversity, the upside to our new region was getting to make friends with students whose families were from Puerto Rico, Japan, Laos, Cambodia, and other parts of the world.

Walking home with my Iranian American friend, Shireen, after school one afternoon, she told me about her parents' divorce. I had met her when she transferred to my school midyear, having left her mother's house in Los Angeles to join her siblings at her father's apartment. I listened to her unemotionally list the reasons why her parents had separated.

"My parents would never get divorced," I responded. "They love each other too much." I wasn't bragging; it was a fact, a universal truth. Above all else, Mom and Dad were bound by an unbreakable spiritual connection.

I'd always found the story of how my parents met to be the most romantic of any love story. Mom was raised in Vermont and hadn't yet left home when she met my father. Dad was a nomadic hippie who took odd jobs across the country from the East Coast to Colorado, all the way to San Francisco, and back again. Dad eventually wound up in Vermont, where he befriended Mom's older brother, Paul, and became a regular at their house. The two men attended worship together at the nearby ashram. This was how Dad came to know Mom, who was a natural beauty at just sixteen years of age.

While Paul eventually lost interest in going to the ashram, Dad continued visiting Mom. They would go for bike rides together. When Mom adopted Dad's spiritual practices, their bond continued to deepen.

My mother became pregnant at seventeen, after which Dad married her. A justice of the peace officiated the ceremony in chambers in October of 1973, attended only by Mom's siblings, Gloria and Paul, who also served as signed witnesses. Afterward, one of them snapped the wedding portrait of Dad in his denim and Mom shyly posing with her arm linked through his. She wore a bell-sleeved persimmon-colored muslin dress with saffron embroidery along the neckline and wrists. Her golden hair hung well past her shoulders, and she was fresh-faced and lovely. Still in her first trimester, Mom's belly didn't show visible evidence that my sister Karina was on the way. Though my grandparents were displeased at the time about the pregnancy and wedding, they came around eventually.

With their union official, my parents moved to rural North Carolina where Dad got work in a glove factory.

In photos of their first years together, my parents looked perfectly at peace. They had accomplished that most daunting task: finding one's soulmate amongst the billions of people on this planet and starting a happy family.

Dad captured a remarkably meditative series of photos of Mom holding two-year-old Karina under the low-hanging foliage of trees painted cheerily in autumn's bright palette. With golden locks matching those of our mother, my sister had a broad smile on her impish face as she reached up to pluck at the vibrant yellow leaves above her head. Mom was radiant with a smile that revealed how much she delighted in her child.

Chapter 20

Mom began working as a vitamin manager at a health food store, a job that better suited her. Since moving to Eastgate, she had become increasingly impatient and withdrawn, and I went out of my way to avoid her.

Then, out of nowhere, Mom started displaying vigor and humor again when, at the age of thirty-four, she progressed from doing aerobics routines in the privacy of our house to working out regularly at a gym with a personal trainer named Reginald. Shortly thereafter, she startled us by declaring her intent to compete in a bodybuilding competition. When I later asked Dad in private how he felt about the announcement, all he said was, "I don't believe in the glorification of the human body."

Completely caught off guard by Mom's bizarre new pursuit, I couldn't relate to the direction she was taking in life. However, her fitness obsession inadvertently benefited my siblings and me when Ben and I discovered our rental house came with cable already connected.

We started watching programs in secret on the TV Mom had purchased for her workouts. Each afternoon following our ten-minute walk home from school, Ben and I would make ourselves peanut butter and jelly sandwiches to eat while enjoying Disney Afternoon cartoons. When Mom eventually caught on, she was adamant about limiting our screen time. My parents hadn't intended to ever let us watch TV, which my father referred to as the "idiot box."

Back in Vermont, we'd had a massive television set from the late seventies, the kind with large knobs and a speaker offset to one side of the screen. But lacking even the most basic cable package, it could only be used to watch movies on weekends. Dad tended to rent slapstick comedies like the Marx Brothers' *Horse Feathers* and *Young Einstein*, while Mom preferred that we watch films based on real life. She subjected us to such heart-wrenching dramas as *Mask*, *The Elephant Man*, and *Sophie's Choice*. I got used to keeping a box of tissues in my lap on family movie night, expecting to shed copious tears for the unimaginable suffering endured by so many innocent people.

For the first time, at the age of thirteen, I was getting to watch TV, like all my friends. It became of the utmost importance to follow *Beverly Hills 90210* like the other girls at school. However, since the hour-long show started at eight o'clock on weekday evenings, it meant I could only watch the first half because our strictly enforced bedtime—which hadn't been modified since I was born—was eight thirty.

While we had my mother's fitness regimen to thank for feeling normalized amongst our peers as far as entertainment was concerned, the concept of her focusing all her free time on building muscle was so foreign to me that I largely ignored her progress.

Chapter 21

Hip-hop having replaced Melissa Etheridge on Mom's radio, she coerced me into calling the local music store to ask what the band Naughty by Nature's song title "O.P.P." stood for.

"Uh," said the salesclerk on the other end of the line, "I'm not sure I should say. Do your parents know you're calling?"

"Yes," I said, looking at Mom's mischievous smile as she stood nearby nodding with anticipation. "My mother is actually the one asking me to call."

"All right," he said, sounding uneasy. "It stands for 'Other People's Pussy.'"

"Okay, thanks," I said, hanging up and relaying the message in a hushed tone.

"I knew it!" Mom said, clapping her hands like she'd just won a prize. She was oddly charged.

I felt weirded out by her behavior. I couldn't believe this was the same mother who had once forbidden Karina and me from listening to Madonna's song "Like a Virgin." Back in Vermont, she had threatened to confiscate our mixed tape if she ever heard it again. She would frown when the Dire Straits sang about getting chicks for free and disapproved of the term Violent Femmes as a band name. Yet, suddenly, she was delighted about O.P.P.

Chapter 22

On a Wednesday night in early November of my freshman year, the midpoint of any normal-seeming school week, I'd just brushed my teeth and was headed into the bedroom I shared with Heidi. The door to my parents' room across the hall was ajar.

"Angie," Mom called out from the darkness within.

I placed my hand on the doorknob and, though unable to see anything, leaned into the room.

"We're moving to Issaquah this weekend," Mom said flatly. "You need to say goodbye to your friends at school tomorrow."

"Wait, what?" I froze in the doorway.

"You need to wrap things up at school tomorrow," she said impatiently, as if I were dense. "You'll be starting at Issaquah High on Monday."

"I don't think it works like that," I stammered, trying to make sense of the news. "Things don't happen that quickly."

"Well, just do whatever it is you need to do," she said.

My hand dropped from the doorknob and hung limply at my side like I was holding a heavy weight. I slipped into my room, closing the door quietly behind me. I was unaware that my parents had located a house to purchase. *When was everyone else informed, and why was I told at bedtime?* I wondered. *Why didn't Dad give me the inside scoop before leaving for his night shift?*

Settling into the lower bunk, with Heidi lying silently on the mattress overhead, I considered how attached I'd become to the house we'd been renting for the past year. It was the best life had been since moving to Washington.

I was very happy at my school, enrolled in interesting classes like German and interior design, and had cultivated friendships with a handful of people. Having joined the Eco Club for the opportunity to do good for the environment, I had developed a crush on a fellow member, a senior named Grant Preston. I had been anticipating our friendship to blossom into a relationship as we continued to chat at the weekly group meeting. It was unbearable having that potential severed.

Last I knew, Mom had been planning on asking our landlords if they would be interested in selling us the rental house. She said we'd finally get a cat, which I'd wanted all my life. I was aware of the looming deadline requiring my parents to reinvest $100,000 in real estate or pay back taxes for the sale of our house in Vermont. However, I felt blindsided by my parents for not giving me more time to prepare for such a significant change, and angry at the government for putting us in this bind. It wasn't fair, especially given that my parents hadn't even turned a profit from the sale of the Vermont home. Without attracting multiple buyers, they'd been forced to accept the only offer they received, parting with the entire property, including an established business and all its assets, for a price lower than the house alone was worth. They were beholden to the government by some arbitrary legal code despite their financial losses and continued hardship, leaving them with the demoralizing challenge of finding an impossibly low-priced house. There were no homes for sale in Bellevue within their budget. They had subsequently looked to the undesirable town of Issaquah for an answer.

The next evening when Mom didn't show up for dinner, Dad explained that she'd gone to the new house in order to have a couple of nights to herself. I thought it strange she wanted to be alone and hadn't even said goodbye to us.

On Friday evening Dad went to visit Mom. When he returned, he had an unusually goofy grin on his face.

"Ugh," Karina said under her breath. "You can tell they had sex." She rolled her eyes at me. I wondered how she could know such a thing.

Chapter 23

When Dad came to collect me after school on my final day at Newport High, I dropped heavily into the passenger seat with a sigh. In my lap, I held everything I had cleared out of my locker.

As we departed from the parking lot, tears rolled down my cheeks, and I wiped them away without a sound. Dad didn't say a word. I resented his failure to inquire about my well-being. Perhaps he felt bad, humiliated even, that he had to disappoint his children in this way.

East of Bellevue, the town of Issaquah was spread across a vast pastoral region, its population so small it felt like a ghost town. The main street was lined with false front buildings, reminders that pioneers had developed them in the nineteenth century. Everything there seemed lost to time.

That Saturday when we arrived, I instantly disliked the vibe of the new house from the driveway. The rambler's brown siding was faded and peeling. Located on a highly trafficked road, it was a mystery where all these cars were coming from or heading to given that Issaquah was such a sleepy town.

Mom met us at the front door, her demeanor muted. She followed along while Dad gave Karina and me a tour of the three-bedroom house. My younger siblings immediately set about exploring the overgrown backyard.

In the kitchen, I raised my eyebrows at the avocado-green cabinets clashing with the orange Formica countertops and dark-brown appliances. Water damage around the perimeter of the skylight had left the faded white paint puckered and cracked. The white linoleum squares lining the floor were warped. Mom opened a drawer and yelped upon finding a mouse inside.

From the splintered, sun-bleached planks of the back patio, I could see that the yard was long and narrow, but it was impossible to determine where the property ended. The view was obscured by a tangled mass of craggy trees, waist-high brambles, and dead plants.

I decided that the house must have been put up for sale after someone died there. It seemed to me just the kind of place where an old loner would pass away, their death going unnoticed for several days.

A gloominess hung heavily about the house, perpetuated by the dim lighting, the dark paint, and outdated appliances and fixtures.

"This wallpaper is hideous," Karina said, pointing at the white floral pattern repeating across the black wallpaper in the main bathroom.

"Oh, it's not that bad," Dad countered.

"This place is dank and dingy," I said, as we walked the length of the cave-like hallway.

"It's only because the house has been sitting empty for a long time," Dad said.

Yes, on account of the death that occurred here, I thought.

I wondered why my father was behaving as defensively as if he were the architect himself. Mom remained silent during the walk-through, observing Karina's and my reactions. She would later confess to us in private that she'd hoped we would reinforce her disdain for the house. Not that it did a lick of good, as we had to live there despite our protests. The forlorn property, instead of having been condemned, was our destiny, and there wasn't a damn thing we could do about it.

Dad said at $105,000 the house was a bargain, given its original price tag of $140,000. I grimaced at his idea of a good deal.

The damp chill in the air indicated that the house was underinsulated. Even worse, Dad explained that the river that formed a natural boundary to the rear of the property was supposedly prone to overflowing in the winter after the typical deluge of Pacific Northwest rains. "But I can pile sandbags along the top of the riverbank," he said. I pictured cold, murky water seeping into the house, warping the floors further and ruining our furniture as it lapped around our ankles.

I would have preferred returning to Gloria's basement. Unfortunately, when we moved out, my aunt had taken Mom aside and told her it was the last time we could stay with her.

The reason why this move stunk of failure so badly was that unlike our arrangement in the basement, which we had known to be temporary, this was permanent. It was no replacement for my beloved childhood home.

The next night, Karina and I were organizing our shared bedroom while Heidi established a makeshift bed on the floor and Ben sat on the bed chattering at us. He was wearing an oversized gray-and-blue bulldog-emblazoned Georgetown jersey he'd found at Sears, even though no one in our family participated in or celebrated sports.

"Angie!" Dad snapped, appearing at our door. "Will you pick up those boxes you left in the entryway? Your mother's getting on my case about them." He didn't wait around for an answer, which was just as well since I promptly burst into tears.

I could count on one hand the number of times Dad had scolded me in my entire life. He was always tender with me. My accumulated stress from an unexpected move coupled with the fear of changing schools midyear came out in a flood of dramatic, heaving sobs.

"Don't worry about it, Ang," Karina said, rubbing my back with one hand. "Something else must be bothering Dad. It's not your fault."

To cheer me up, Ben started reciting quotes from his favorite comedies, like *National Lampoon's Christmas Vacation*, doing a spot-on impersonation of the actors who had originally said the lines. I laughed, then cried again. After several minutes I finally wiped my eyes, blew my nose, and returned to putting clothes away in the dresser.

Chapter 24

Mom was supposed to get me enrolled at Issaquah High that Monday afternoon, but her late return from work made us miss the window of opportunity. Neither of my parents prioritized enrolling me over the next few days, so I simply hung out at the house, which was fine by me since I wasn't in any rush to start at a new school.

Karina was the most fortunate of all of us once again: the freedom afforded by having her own car meant she could simply drive herself to school each day. She was a senior at an enviable school where there were no classes with other students, just consultations with teachers, like private tutoring. The unique arrangement enabled her to have longer work shifts at a toy store near campus. She had been able to purchase a burgundy Volkswagen Beetle with black faux fur seat covers with her earnings.

By the end of the first week, I became aware of an alternative high school right next door to Issaquah High. While the latter looked like a prison and had hundreds of students, Horizon's Edge was a small campus of tract buildings that held classes Monday through Thursday between eleven in the morning and six in the evening.

The Horizon's Edge admissions counselor explained these schedule details to Mom and me as we sat in the counselor's office, facing her across a desk with chipped mahogany laminate that exposed the beige particle board underneath. The middle-aged woman had applied blue eyeliner well beneath the lash line of her lower eyelids, making her pale, pudgy face look like a melting wax figure. Her thick brown hair flipped upward in shaggy layers like a pine tree, resting heavily atop her square shoulders. She wore a black blazer over a burgundy button-up shirt, as though to maintain a professional demeanor. However, the coat was of a cheap material that shapelessly bunched around her torso, creating quite the opposite effect.

Mom volunteered the observation that we were an alternative family, so it only made sense for me to attend an alternative school. Then she laughed, looking back and forth between the expressionless admissions counselor and me. I forced a smile. The pleasantries were neither necessary nor reciprocated by the counselor, given that I was accepted on the spot. It became apparent from my first moments as a student that the school accepted anyone.

From day one I liked Horizon's Edge but felt self-conscious about being so different from the other students. The unusual class schedule was designed to accommodate the many students with jobs or unconventional lifestyles. I determined that if I kept a low profile, perhaps these older students with multiple piercings, tattoos, and leather jackets wouldn't perceive me as a misfit Goody Two-shoes.

I had a crush on a seventeen-year-old boy until I witnessed him chewing tobacco in our Pacific Northwest history class. As he spat the juice into a plastic cup in his hand, I averted my gaze. Nick had initially appeared to have his life together. But now he had become, in my eyes, just another one of the many kooky characters at the school. In that same class was a young man known for his loose shoulder-length hair, cargo shorts, and skater shoes who suddenly showed up for class in a suit and ponytail. All the other students hooted and whistled at him and asked, "Why so fancy?" Jeff clutched his lapels like a sheriff from an old Western movie and proudly announced, "I'm due in court this afternoon and want to look nice for the judge."

One day I saw Tammy, the sole person I considered a friend, walking between buildings. I ran to catch up, assuming she was on her way to the smoking section.

"Hey, Tammy!" I called. "It's nice to see you. Where are you headed?"

"Hi, Angie," she said in her usual upbeat manner. She was full-figured, wore a black leather jacket, and kept her brown bob teased and sprayed to maintain volume. "I'm going to visit my daughter at the onsite daycare. Wanna come?"

My jaw dropped, but I quickly shut it before she noticed. I was between classes and, with nowhere else to hang out, accepted her invitation. As Tammy sat on the foam floor mat playing with her toddler, I kept a smile plastered on my face as I awkwardly perched on a child-sized chair nearby. Mentally chastising myself for being a third wheel, I felt even more out of place there than anywhere else on campus.

Having ignored all previous clues, I now had undeniable proof that Tammy wasn't a child like me. She was not only a senior but also a real woman. She was old enough to buy her own Marlboros legally and had become my source during my early foray into smoking, which should have tipped me off. She had far bigger concerns than homework, and it was clear that our friendship was never going to carry over into the weekends. I thought back to the time she explained how she used three different perfumes: a sweet scent on her neck to reel 'em in, musk in her cleavage to take things to the next level, and a floral scent on her wrists for her own enjoyment. In retrospect, this habit seemed to have been exactly what got her into trouble in the first place, and my private conclusion was that she should just leave the perfumes on the dresser.

I had started craving cigarettes out of nowhere, believing they would help relieve stress, and took up smoking whenever Tammy gave me a few. I kept the loose cigarettes in my jacket, which left the filters coated with pocket lint. The irony wasn't lost on me as I tediously picked off the lint with surgical precision despite knowing the cigarette itself was carcinogenic.

After finishing a cigarette on the patio one evening, I walked into the kitchen where my mother sat at the table alone reading a bodybuilding magazine. It was easy to forget she was still preparing for a competition since, with her clothes on, she didn't appear muscular. She had stopped eating the meals that Dad prepared for the family, adopting a strict reduced-carbohydrate diet instead.

I slowly navigated past my mother, expecting my smoky stench to waft her way. She didn't look up, so I crossed the kitchen again. I started to feel impatient that no one had taken notice that I'd become a smoker, and I wanted my parents to show concern.

"Do I smell like anything to you?" I asked.

"No," Mom said disinterestedly.

"I've been smoking," I announced.

"That's disgusting," she said, looking up momentarily. "And it'll give you premature wrinkles."

Chapter 25

Shortly after the move to Issaquah, my teddy bear hamster passed away. I sensed it was Gus's last night on earth when his usual frenetic movements became exaggeratedly slow. I smiled at him through his glass cage, like a mother who loves her child with all her heart and fights to remain positive for his sake despite knowing he isn't well.

Dad had made pasta for dinner, and I placed a piece of tomato-sauce-topped rigatoni before Gus. He sat up on his haunches, gently pulling the noodle upright between his paws, and began to nibble it with his eyes half closed. It took him a long time to finish the meal. I continued monitoring him as he wobbled into his bed, curled up amongst the cotton fluff, and went to sleep.

In the morning, the first thing I did was check on Gus. He was still curled up in his bed. I gently stroked his soft golden fur and felt that his body was cold and lifeless. I was grateful he had gotten to enjoy a good dinner before passing away.

It was bad timing for his death though. I had expected to bury him beneath the cherry tree in the backyard at our family's former house. Each spring, the tree at the rental property blossomed in a gorgeous display of nature at its finest. I couldn't picture a more ideal spot for a grave, where fresh bouquets of pale-pink blossoms would be deposited.

Burying Gus outside our new house wasn't an option. Heidi, having interred her own deceased hamster there a few weeks earlier, was traumatized the next morning to find that a scavenger had exhumed the tiny corpse and likely eaten it for a midnight snack. I was adamant that my precious pet be laid to rest in the peaceful spot I had preselected for him, which presented a significant challenge given that we no longer lived there.

"Just put him in the garbage can," Mom suggested.

"No!" I squealed. "He's going to get a proper burial."

Since she was the only person with transportation who could be convinced to help me achieve my goal, I set about pleading with Karina. I already had Gus nestled inside his bed-turned-coffin and a shovel ready for the journey. "It will be a quick in-and-out job," I assured my sister.

After school, we loaded the miniature coffin and shovel into the back seat of Karina's burgundy Beetle and set out to accomplish the task. To my horror, the floodlights above the garage at the rental property were on, which implied there were new occupants. My hopes were dashed as we passed without stopping.

Karina, sensing my despair, assured me we would try again the following day. With the coffin and shovel still sitting in her car, she drove us to the old house again twenty-four hours later. When we found the outside lights still on, we returned home defeated once more.

The next afternoon, I asked Karina if we were going to do a third drive-by. She surprised me by saying she'd already gone to our old house directly after school. Deciding that enough was enough, she'd dashed into the backyard with the coffin and shovel in hand, quickly buried Gus beneath the cherry tree, and sped off before anyone could have the chance to ask what she was doing there.

The risk Karina had taken on my behalf was heartwarming. Through her selfless act, she had given me the gift of closure.

Chapter 26

Dad enlisted my help brightening up the kitchen walls with a fresh coat of white paint. Meanwhile, Mom demonstrated no interest in decorating or otherwise putting her touch on the house. The only decisive action she took was to bring home a black cat from the humane society, which she named, very simply, Kitty.

From hearing the story many times, we all knew Mom had had a black cat as a teenager that she loved dearly and had never gotten over losing. And now, it was mystifying to me why she hadn't brought any of her children along to select a pet together. Instead, she made what should have been a joyous family affair all about herself. I had pleaded with her for years to let me get a cat, but her answer was always the same: "When Ryan is older." With my little brother's unpredictability in temper tantrums, she felt it wasn't a good idea to bring a pet into the home. I resented him for this. I'd finally stopped asking, and though Ryan's temperament hadn't improved, Mom adopted a cat anyway.

Kitty was a most welcome addition to the family since her presence lent a sense of normalcy to what otherwise felt anything but normal. However, the worst thing about our new domicile was revealed after Kitty's arrival, when the half-inch gap under the patio door permitted banana slugs to invade the kitchen. Nightmarish creatures—as long and thick as an adult finger, in shades of brown or black or orange—wriggled their way in, leaving tell-tale trails of slime across the linoleum. Whenever Kitty discovered them curled over the top of her food bowl partaking of her meal, she recoiled and walked away without eating.

Chapter 27

One evening as Dad prepared dinner, Ben and I were squabbling in the kitchen.

"You never do anything around here!" I scolded my brother as I set the table.

"I've mowed the lawn before!" he retorted.

"Yeah, all of *one* time!"

"Would you guys knock it off!" Dad growled.

We turned to look at him in surprise.

"My father just died today, all right?" He flung the ladle he was holding into the pot on the stove and left the kitchen.

Ben and I stared at each other, speechless. I continued setting the table in silence.

Although we'd only gotten to visit Granddad a couple of times given that he lived in Louisiana, I loved him. It hurt that Dad chose to inform us of such significant news in a way that was disrespectful to both Granddad's memory and us.

In addition to the emotional complexity Dad was clearly struggling to manage, having lost a father with whom he wasn't particularly close due to unresolved issues, money was so tight that he wasn't even able to join his brothers at the funeral.

Chapter 28

Looking for a snack to tide me over until dinner one evening, I found Dad in the kitchen cooking with a sour expression on his face.

"What's wrong?" I asked as I popped a slice of cucumber into my mouth.

"Your mother cheated on me," he said flatly.

"What? No!" I exclaimed, swallowing unchewed pulp. I didn't know where Dad had gotten such an idea, but it was preposterous. I headed for my parents' bedroom to check on Mom.

Tapping gently, I opened the door to find her sitting slumped at the edge of the bed weeping softly. *They must have had a misunderstanding*, I thought. With Karina away at work, it was up to me to comfort my mother. But I had no intention of repeating Dad's outlandish claim.

"I'm sorry you feel sad, Mom," I said, taking a seat next to her and placing my hand on her back awkwardly. "I'd like for us to be friends."

She nodded, wiping her eyes. "I would like that too," she said, her voice cracking.

I felt hopeful for an improved relationship with Mom. Karina had been taking her out regularly after work, just the two of them. I was annoyed by their exclusive club, but more so about the fact that Mom didn't show the slightest interest in me so long as she had my older sister in her corner. The two of them had always enjoyed an easy way about their conversations, given that Mom preferred the company of people she could talk to at her level. I imagined they were having a great deal of fun as they wouldn't return until after eleven o'clock at night, laughing and talking too loudly. It was always disruptive for the rest of us who had already gone to bed.

Chapter 29

That Thanksgiving, Mom took my siblings and me to Gloria's house, where there wasn't much we could eat beyond sweet potato casserole and green beans. Dad didn't specify why he wasn't joining us. I attributed it to the fact that he didn't like Gloria.

Why aren't we having a family dinner at home like we always have? I wondered.

Our first Thanksgiving in Washington had felt much the same as our Vermont celebration. As usual, it had been just our family, and we'd feasted on a medley of vegetable casseroles, roasted chestnut stuffing, and Mom's special ambrosia salad made with vegan marshmallows.

By this point in the year, the air should have felt charged with Christmas just around the corner. But with Dad's absence, something didn't feel right.

The answer became apparent as soon as our Christmas tree went up when, instead of us all spending time basking in front of our glowing seasonal guest, Mom called a family meeting.

My parents each stood to one side of the tree. Dad was silent, an emotion I'd never seen before tensing his face and darkening his eyes.

"Your father and I are separating," Mom said.

How is this possible? I wondered. Reeling from the unexpected turn of events, I felt betrayed by them both. This meant my parents weren't a cohesive unit as I'd assumed; they were in fact two very different people seeking different things out of life. It also indicated that Mom really had cheated on Dad.

"When?" Karina asked.

"We don't know yet," Mom said. "There are a lot of details to sort out. But soon."

I was speechless. After the announcement, I ushered Karina into our bedroom and closed the door.

"Can you believe this is happening?" I asked her with tears in my eyes.

"It's no surprise, Ang," she said, pulling her car keys from her pocket and setting them on the dresser. "Dad has been sleeping on the couch at night."

"He has?"

"And haven't you noticed that Mom and Dad aren't talking?" she continued, hanging her jacket in the closet.

"Well, I have noticed they never seem to be in the same room anymore," I said, dropping heavily into a seated position at the edge of the bed. "But that doesn't mean the same thing as overhearing arguments. I've never heard them fight." I watched Karina lay out her outfit for the next day.

"This was a long time coming," she said, with the wisdom of an older sister.

Once I thought more about it, I realized that ever since we'd moved into the new house, Mom hadn't been around much. When she was home, she was reading bodybuilding magazines in the kitchen or living room— anywhere Dad wasn't. I didn't see her cook or clean, and she certainly wasn't spending time with my siblings and me. But since Dad was always present—outside of work hours—cooking and cleaning, it didn't faze me that Mom wasn't. Even while continuing to bulk up physically, she'd faded into the background, rarely joining the rest of the family when we were in the common areas.

I no longer saw any evidence of certain behaviors that had been commonplace in Vermont. Mom used to seek Dad out for long, exaggerated hugs and, if she was especially full of pluck, would insist on giving him a piggyback ride around the living room. He would assume a resigned look on his face, and we kids would giggle uncontrollably as we watched Mom hoist him onto her back and clomp around the perimeter.

I could always tell when Dad was content, rocking back and forth on his toes and snapping his fingers. Sometimes he whistled a tune as well. He also kept an array of funny masks. His favorite was a rubber gorilla head, which he donned before leaping out from behind corners to get a rise out of his kids.

Not only had this playful behavior my parents once exhibited stopped, but also our family fell out of the habit of eating dinner together, given that Mom and Dad had been avoiding each other, Karina worked late most evenings, and my younger siblings spent so much of their time at friends' houses. The most important tradition we had as a family was taking our meals together around our special dining table. For the first time, I felt lonely. I didn't know it was possible to feel that way when you had a large family.

Back in Vermont, my parents had intentionally segregated our family as part of our faith. In fact, Dad had always made a big point of telling us that he and Mom had moved to Heathburn from North Carolina, where I was born, expressly so their children could attend school at Satmardeva. The haven my parents created for us in New England was once-in-a-lifetime and couldn't be sustained without the support of that community. There were very few pockets of our belief system across the world, limiting the number of places we could count on to find others like us.

After the cross-country move, we were left without the ability to attend Sunday services. As our focus had been on settling into our new surroundings, I didn't think much about it at first. But it was now apparent that no longer having dedicated time for a spiritual connection had had a detrimental impact on our family, and we were experiencing the fallout.

My parents had been unable to recreate what we'd had in Vermont: we didn't have a permanent home like the one we'd left that could comfortably accommodate our large family, we didn't have a special school or like-minded community, and we didn't have a place to worship. All we had was our family, and now we were on the verge of losing that too.

Chapter 30

My English teacher at Horizon's Edge doubled as the school's counselor, and I began seeing her on a weekly basis. In addition to being sad, I loathed being alone, especially at night. All my happy childhood memories were tinged with bitterness now that it was clear we had given everything up for nothing. Everything Mom had told us about why we should move was a lie to support her own selfish desires. Without a distraction, these memories replayed in my mind on a continuous loop.

Shirley was a heavyset woman with short-cropped brown hair framing her disinterested face, which communicated loud and clear that she'd seen and heard it all. Though a nice enough teacher, Shirley wasn't particularly skilled as a counselor, failing to provide useful tips on how to incite change in an unhappy home. She cut me off once, right as I was complaining about how my mother treated me like I was "unsuperior."

"Inferior," Shirley corrected, nodding her head.

My chain of thought was replaced with embarrassment at having accidentally used a non-word in front of my English teacher.

I told Shirley how my unexpected craving for cigarettes seemed impossible given that neither of my parents were smokers and no one had pressured me into smoking.

"Peer pressure doesn't just come from another person coercing you to do something," Shirley said. "It also comes from what you see around you, in person, on television, and in advertising."

Chapter 31

At the pinnacle of her physical transformation from the mother I'd known in Vermont, Mom was like a butterfly testing the strength of its dewy wings for the first time. But who's to say that what emerges from the cocoon is more beautiful than what went in?

Having spent the better part of a year preparing to participate in a bodybuilding competition, during which Mom significantly reduced her body fat by maintaining a diet of low-fat, high-protein meals centered around rehydrated black bean flakes, she had packed on an astonishing layer of muscle.

Finally, the time came for the competition.

Mom called me into the bathroom one morning, insistent that I baste her backside with a sunless tanning solution the consistency of soy sauce. This was standard practice for light-skinned contestants, she said, to highlight muscle definition. Having already painted her front half herself, she stood in the bathtub nude while I employed a flat foam brush—the kind house painters use for finer details—to coat the entire back half of her body from her neck down to her heels.

"This isn't how I want to spend my Saturday," I complained.

"Just be careful to apply a perfectly even layer," Mom instructed. "I'll get Deandra to do it next time."

Deandra was Mom's coworker from the health food store and also a bodybuilder. As I patted the foam brush across my mother's buttocks, I wondered how much influence Deandra had had on Mom's single-minded focus on this strange mission.

The level of dedication Mom had demonstrated to achieving her goal was remarkable. She was driven to an extent I had never witnessed from anyone before. This awareness did nothing for me, however, in the way of counteracting the deeply unsettling nature of beholding my mother's nude muscular frame and artificially darkened skin.

Through Karina, I learned that we were invited to attend the competition. I emphatically declined.

"She's worked so hard for this," my sister implored. "The least we can do is cheer her on."

Though I had steadfastly refused to provide positive reinforcement for the metamorphosis Mom was undergoing, I begrudgingly consented to the invitation. I didn't want to fall out of favor with Karina if I didn't oblige.

The revulsion I felt about the unwholesome transition came to a head as Mom drove my sister and me to the venue. She confided in us that her personal trainer Reginald was her lover. It turned out that the night I'd comforted Mom after finding her weeping on her bed had in fact been when she'd confessed to Dad.

Mom proceeded to describe her first sexual encounter with this man. It had occurred in the passenger seat of that very same car. She talked of how absurd it was as the two of them tried to fit into such a cramped space, with Reginald as tall and muscular as he was. I foresaw how this unwelcome image would be revisited upon me every time I rode in the car, and I was grateful to be sitting in the back seat as these details unfolded so I could frown and keep silent.

When we arrived at the Moore Theatre in Seattle, Reginald came out to the lobby to greet my mother. Threading an arm around her back, he kissed her on the cheek.

"Reggie, I'd like you to meet my daughters," Mom said, with a big smile. Her tone was buoyant with pride. "This is Karina and Angie."

Her trainer was a six-foot-tall Black man with a shaved head, chunky biceps that the sleeves of his tight gray T-shirt struggled to contain, and a surprisingly gentle voice. I felt compelled by social conventions to shake the hand of the man who'd played a part in destroying my family. It was soft and warm. Beckoning for us to follow him, he led us to a reserved row close to the stage. As I took my seat, I glowered with resentment at having been forced to meet Reginald. I felt I ought to have contempt for him, a homewrecker. On the other hand, he couldn't be blamed; it was in truth all my mother's doing.

There we were, two minors sitting at the foot of the stage upon which bulky men in swim briefs and women in string bikinis confidently strutted about before the competition got underway.

Despite their heavy application of lipstick and eye shadow, the female contestants had lost their natural femininity, and many of them appeared to have undergone breast augmentation to compensate for having shed all their body fat. Through the barely-there bikinis, I could see the outlines of their pectoral muscles, upon each of which a perky breast sat like a scoop of ice cream on top of a pancake. Of the lot, Mom looked the most natural, which was ironic given how much she had changed over such a short period of time.

My skin crawled as I witnessed the rampant display of human flesh, so lumpy and grotesque—the hairless, oiled bodies shining as they promenaded beneath the floodlights. Nothing about this bizarre scene seemed right to me. Dad's disapproving words about the "glorification of the human body" loomed heavily in my mind.

Karina and I had to sit through the heavyweight category in order to watch Mom compete in middleweight. My sister whooped and clapped as soon as our mother crossed the stage wearing a burgundy bikini and with her hair pulled back in a perfect French braid. It was surreal seeing her up there in the spotlight, exposed before an audience. She proceeded through her routine, the same motions as all the other contestants before her, striking poses that illuminated the biceps, the deltoids, and the calves. She pivoted to turn her backside to the room, squeezing her arms down from above her head with clenched fists. I glanced around, uncomfortably. All the viewers surrounding me were smiling as though this were perfectly normal.

Mom didn't end up placing. "I should have registered in the lightweight category," she repeated over and over on the drive home.

"Mom, you did great out there," Karina said. "You looked incredible."

With no trophy to reward her efforts, my mother's interest in bodybuilding waned. In time, the sunless tanning solution wore off, and I was relieved for the madness to be over.

Chapter 32

"Your mother has left," Dad unceremoniously announced one evening, his voice wavering. My younger siblings and I froze in place as we stood collected in the living room.

"I wanna go with Mom!" Ryan declared.

"She doesn't want you kids," Dad said, quashing my little brother's sentiment.

We gathered close, clutching our remaining parent with our arms. The notion of my parents' marriage truly being over was unthinkable. I'd hoped that continuing to cohabitate would encourage reconciliation between them.

I felt a quivering desperation inside my chest, a sensation of falling while flailing my arms in an attempt to gain stability. I couldn't believe Mom had actually left. *Love is supposed to solve everything*, I thought.

There was no trace that my mother had ever occupied the house. It was as though from the moment she'd moved in, she'd been planning her escape.

She'd left Kitty behind in order to avoid paying a pet deposit at her new apartment. I wondered why she would adopt a cat just to abandon the poor thing so soon after.

For several weeks, my younger siblings and I were overly attached to Dad, hugging him constantly and pig-piling on top of him as he lay on his bed to read. His sad face and drooping shoulders made me feel protective of him.

Obsessed with the notion that if my parents were to reconcile, everything would return to normal, I fantasized about getting them back together as the children did in the old Disney film *The Parent Trap*. As though sensing my plot, Dad adopted a stern new refrain: "Me and your mother aren't getting back together." Regardless, I was convinced it was a trial separation.

Recalling how the paper dolls I used to play with could so easily transition from one lifestyle to the next, I determined that real life must have the same potential. If we didn't like how the new lifestyle turned out, we could always revert to how things had been before. In the worst-case scenario, my siblings and I would have the benefit of duplicates to look forward to. Children of divorce got bedrooms in two different houses, double the holidays, double the gifts, and double the attention as each parent endeavored to outdo the other.

Chapter 33

As if on cue, Dad began a rigorous campaign of spoiling me. He seemed to have money to burn, repeatedly making impractical purchases like a blow-up pool for the backyard. It was out of character; for as long as I'd known him, he had been frugal. Whenever my siblings and I had asked for money to buy the name-brand clothing that was in style at school, Dad would tell us how he purchased all his clothing from Costco for wallet-friendly prices.

"I bought the pants I'm wearing right now for five dollars," he once boasted.

Which is why they look like part of a mechanic's uniform, I thought.

We didn't want off-brand clothing; we wanted to fit in. But once Dad started reciting each of his clothing items' bargain prices, it signified the end of the conversation.

However, now he was regularly taking me to eat dinner at Bite of India in the Crossroads Mall, watch movies at the theater where Karina used to work, and shopping from a gourmet grocery store where I purchased copious quantities of chocolate.

At first, I didn't question this new dynamic as I was pleased to have the attention and all the opportunities to get out of the house. However, cutting comments from my siblings about how I was clearly Dad's favorite made me realize that, while they were permitted to come along on our excursions, my father's invitations were extended only to me. It also occurred to me that I was receiving the type of treatment Mom had always desired from Dad and, worse, that my father was likely hoping to make her jealous. Out of concern that the knowledge would hurt Mom, I refrained from informing her of my unprecedented new lifestyle.

In the kitchen alone with Dad one evening, he unexpectedly lifted my hand and put his wedding ring in my palm. I looked at him quizzically.

"I'm not married anymore," he announced, as though it were sufficient explanation. "I burned my marriage certificate on the patio."

I pictured my father standing over a metal bucket, eagerly watching flames reduce the binding document to weightless bits of ash.

To delay making eye contact, I held my upturned palm close enough to study the design etched into the ring. Whereas I once thought it resembled an infinite vine, I now realized it looked more like waves. Determined waves, the kind that snatch sunbathers' possessions off a beach and abandon them in the vast, lonely center of the sea.

That Dad chose me to inherit his ring made me feel honored yet also inexplicably perturbed. Not knowing what else to do, I slipped it onto the thumb of my right hand and mumbled an obligatory thank you.

Chapter 34

At a local craft store, I discovered a kit for an enormous Victorian dollhouse, just like one that had captivated me at the library in the next town over from where we had lived in Vermont. The dollhouse was kept in the children's section, and every feature down to the smallest detail had been obsessed over to create an accurate replica of a wealthy Victorian family. Tiny realistic dolls were placed in various rooms throughout the two-story home: one was cooking in the kitchen, another sleeping in bed, and a third sitting to read in the parlor.

No matter that I was now fourteen—I wanted this similar model desperately. But at eighty dollars, it not only cost a prohibitive amount but also was an irresponsible way to spend money. When no amount of logic could quiet my desire, I begged Dad to purchase the kit, promising to help out any way I could to earn it. Surprisingly, it didn't take as much effort to convince him as expected.

Upon bringing it home, I opened the box on top of the children's play table in our living room and set about sorting the beige die-cut wooden pieces. They hadn't been buffed or varnished and were unpleasant to the touch, especially when I grazed my wrists over the tops of the walls once they were erected.

I aspired to fill the house with miniatures—a family of porcelain dolls and realistic furniture. I already had a head start on the furnishings, having received several pieces from my grandmother over the years. There was an old-fashioned stove made of black steel, a fireplace, a dresser, and a bathtub. I still needed to acquire the dolls, a dining table, and beds, which would take time since such items were expensive. Eager to see the project brought to completion, all my spare time and energy was channeled into this one activity.

Ben had his friend Trevor over after school while I was hard at work in the living room.

"Look at my sister," Ben said, with a smirk. "She's fourteen, and she's got a dollhouse!"

Ever since the film *Terminator 2* had premiered, he had been growing out his spiky light-brown hair like the actor Edward Furlong. His bangs now swept low across his face, so he had to keep bucking his head to get them to fall to the side. Now that he had a hairstyle to show off, gone was the Georgetown cap that had once been a permanent fixture on his head.

"I'm building this for my little sister!" I blurted, meeting Trevor's green eyes.

I felt myself blushing and hoped he couldn't tell. To my relief he smiled and didn't say anything, apparently not wanting to get involved in a sibling dispute. Only after they had disappeared into Ben's room did I resume my work, muttering to myself about how mean-spirited it had been of my brother to embarrass me like that in front of his cute friend. The fact that Trevor was younger than me didn't help soften the blow to my ego.

Either I wasn't following the instructions correctly or key pieces were missing from the kit. After weeks of construction, I found myself unable to complete the roof. What sagged before me on the table didn't look at all like the stately Victorian house pictured on the box. My version, in its unfinished state, with incomplete furnishings and missing family, looked like a house that had fallen into disrepair. It was a lost cause, and I soon abandoned the project.

⌒

As Dad's frenetic purchasing activity waged on, he acquired the most luxurious nonessential of all: an espresso machine. He quickly became as skilled as a seasoned barista, which wasn't surprising given how he mastered any kitchen undertaking.

"Do you want coconut or vanilla syrup today?" Dad would ask.

Because the machine could only make two lattes at a time, he didn't offer them to anyone but me. It was a decadent treat, and it made me feel special to be given coffee.

At first, the buying spree had been a fun diversion from the realities of our broken home, but after the novelty wore off, I became alarmed by Dad's lack of self-control. I felt compelled to inquire how he was suddenly able to afford all these things.

"I inherited twenty thousand dollars from my father," he said, "and I don't want your mother getting her hands on it, or she'll spend it all on herself."

It was a terribly mean-spirited thing to say. I felt guilty about having reaped the benefits of what was akin to blood money. He had, he said, first paid down some of their shared credit card debt, but it seemed glaringly hypocritical that he was frittering away the rest of the money just as he accused my mother of being likely to do.

Chapter 35

As more time went by, Dad's sorrow converted entirely into bitterness. Perhaps the permanence of the new living arrangement had sunk in when Karina joined Mom at her apartment to be closer to school and work.

With Karina gone, the boys took over the room I'd shared with her, and Dad took the smallest room, putting Heidi and me into the primary bedroom. Since I'd outgrown playing with her, I wasn't sure what to do with a roommate five years my junior who liked to copy my interests.

I felt overwhelmed by the constant reminders of my siblings' mental anguish that our parents weren't addressing. I resented Mom and Dad when I discovered Heidi weeping on our bed. Clutching the pastel-green blankie she'd had since infancy, she said she wasn't getting hugged enough.

Ryan and Heidi's squabbles were growing ever worse. Though I did my best to play peacemaker, Ryan constantly terrorized his older sister who would scream at ear-splitting volumes as he chased her around the house yelling, "I'll kill you!" It would escalate into real physical violence whenever Dad wasn't there to intervene. Heidi fought back as good as she got, and it being surrounded by such rage was unsettling. I couldn't bear to hear the shouting and witness the pummeling and scratching.

My little brother had an unnatural temper like no child I'd ever seen. On one occasion when he was at his worst, though I commanded my siblings to stop fighting, they didn't hear me over their screeching. I yelled louder, and they continued to ignore my presence. Finally, I pushed my way between them, placing one hand on each of their chests to hold them apart. Ryan took a swing at Heidi and wound up punching me in the gut. The blow was forceful for a small child.

"You asshole!" I shouted. As I stormed off to my bedroom to nurse my pride, the shock of what had just gone down brought an abrupt end to their quarrel. It was the only time I'd ever been struck in my life, and the blow was dealt by a seven-year-old.

Ryan found other ways to act up as well. Our elderly neighbor alerted Dad to having caught my brother throwing rocks at his RV's headlights. He came to ask my father to pay for replacements and suggested that he give his son a good spanking. I was standing in the hallway, just out of sight, eavesdropping on the conversation taking place at the front door. I heard Dad promise the neighbor that he would be reimbursed and Ryan would be disciplined. After the man left, however, Dad didn't so much as interact with Ryan. While I certainly didn't want any of my siblings to be the recipient of physical punishment, I was surprised Dad didn't even scold his errant son. Either he felt like Ryan was a lost cause, or he was simply too depressed to do anything about it.

Chapter 36

When Dad stopped taking me out, I was relieved. I didn't want him to continue buying me unnecessary gifts if they weren't offered to my siblings as well.

Out of boredom on weekend nights, I spent hours uninterrupted in my en suite bathroom, primping and preening. After applying lipstick, I would test which eye shadow best matched it and style my long brown hair in different ways. Scrutinizing myself in the mirror, I assessed that my smile was unattractive on account of my crooked teeth and how the corners of my mouth curved downward, revealing my lack of confidence.

I did feel good about my slender eyebrows, however, which had been permanently shaped when, at the age of eight, I put on a show to cheer up Ben. He, a rowdy six-year-old, had been sent to his room for bad behavior. I was in the backyard when I observed Ben peering glumly out of his bedroom window. His chubby cheeks were propped up in his hands, and my immediate inclination was to make him laugh.

Climbing on top of the picnic table in my brother's line of sight, I began to dance in the silly fashion of Groucho Marx from the film *Horse Feathers*. I stooped low, flapped my elbows, and waddled back and forth across the table.

Encouraged by my brother's smile, I decided to take my performance up a notch. I pulled a blob of Hubba Bubba gum out of my mouth, tore it in two, and pressed the spittle-moistened pink goo onto each of my eyebrows. Then I waggled my brows up and down, continuing the absurd dance.

The big payoff was seeing Ben laugh until his cheeks turned pink. My work was complete.

After the proverbial curtains closed, I found that the gum didn't pop off as easily as I'd expected. It had dried out. My mother used tweezers to pull it off bit by bit, but despite her best efforts, the gum took hair with it just as waxing would do, and it never grew back.

∞

I liked to mix and match different pieces from my wardrobe, challenging myself to create a trendy ensemble. My favorite was a knee-length black denim skirt, a fuchsia camisole under a loosely crocheted black top I'd purchased to copy my friend Shireen's enviable alternative wardrobe, and a jean jacket passed down to me from Karina. Regardless of the combination of makeup, clothing, and hairstyle, I never felt like I was quite pulling it off.

When it got late, I would remove all the makeup, put on my pajamas, and get into bed. My most consistent source of company was Kitty. I appreciated having her around; her silent watchfulness was comforting. Although it couldn't have been intentional on Mom's part, it felt like a motherly token had been left for me in the form of this loving cat.

The last thing I would see before turning off the light and going to sleep in my parents' old bed was a photo I had taken of them right before we left Vermont. During our final summer in 1989, I had asked my parents to pose for me on the patio. Dad was wearing an old T-shirt, jeans, and sneakers, and Mom, a white T-shirt, denim skirt, and Birkenstock sandals. As usual Mom's hair was parted straight down the middle and tucked behind her ears, and she wore no makeup or jewelry.

"Move a few inches to your right," I had instructed my parents. They shuffled shoulder to shoulder with their backs against the wall like middle school students at their first dance. Rather than putting an arm around each other, Mom clasped her hands behind her back with a shy smile while Dad folded his arms across his chest which he puffed up like a saluting military commander. The restrained smile beneath his half-closed eyes indicated self-consciousness. I had inherited the same sleepy smile.

"Okay, stay there," I said, giggling at my parents' awkwardness as I raised the camera to my eye.

I was glad that I'd orchestrated the photo, despite it making my parents self-conscious at the time. I kept it pinned to the wall with a six-inch-long strip of black lace draped across the top to form a shroud.

I missed summer dinners in Vermont taken at the picnic table in our yard. I used to shuck corn on the front porch with my siblings, tossing the rough green leaves and silken yellow strands into a paper sack. Dad would boil the corncobs and serve them with fried tofu, greens, rolls, and watermelon. We'd finish every summer meal with coffee ice cream. Meanwhile, fireflies with their mysterious self-generated light created a magical backdrop. There were no fireflies in Washington, and summer just wasn't the same without them.

Chapter 37

Eventually, Dad informed Mom of his inheritance money. He told her that if they were still together, he would have turned the entire check over to her to determine the best use of the unexpected funds. This struck me as an awfully spiteful thing to say.

Through phone conversations with Mom, I learned that she had exited the marriage because Dad was emotionally unavailable. Each time she complained that things weren't working, Dad had promised to change, but after a couple weeks, he would backslide into his old habits. There had never been any romance in their relationship, according to her; it was merely a partnership for running a business and child-rearing.

My parents' marriage, which I'd believed throughout my childhood to be a solid, unbreakable symbol for timeless love, had turned out to be nothing more than a house of cards on a tightrope. How had I misread it so badly? Yet, in retrospect, how could such a marriage have stood the test of time? My father, seven years' Mom's senior, had already gotten to travel the country enjoying his freedom as a hippie, whereas my mother went directly from an unhappy childhood home to living with my father and a baby. Mom's story, as she told it now, was that Dad had only married her because he got her pregnant out of wedlock when she was seventeen. They didn't even get along on their wedding day, though she couldn't remember why. I imagined it had something to do with her parents' refusal to attend the ceremony. In my parents' case, first came love, then came the baby in the baby carriage, then came the obligatory, ill-fated marriage.

Mom had five children by the time she was twenty-eight, each of them unplanned. It now made sense why she'd turned to self-help books for an answer. When those failed to deliver, she followed her desires wherever they led—away from her marriage, faith, children, and ideals.

I had never heard my parents speak ill of each other before, and the very fact that they now engaged in dragging each other's names through the mud was almost more shocking than the words themselves. It made me sick to my stomach, and I wanted it to stop. But it didn't stop, because even though Mom had moved out, she still had resentments about my father that she wanted to share with her children, while simultaneously too preoccupied with a thriving dating scene to address our emotional needs. Likewise, Dad's priority was to protect himself, hurt first by his wife leaving him and then receiving what he interpreted as unwarranted verbal attacks from his emotionally distraught children.

I resolved to help my parents see the error of their ways with my impassioned speeches on the irreparable damage they were doing to each other and their children. This only made things worse.

As the relationship between Dad and his children further degraded, he adopted a new refrain: "I can't wait until you kids turn eighteen and move out!"

Refusing to accept any responsibility for our torment, he withdrew like a hermit crab.

"When I have kids someday, I'm going to raise them right!" I told my father after a particularly heated discussion.

"Good luck with that," he retorted.

When I lacked the courage to tell Dad to his face exactly how he was failing as a parent, I described my disappointment in letters. I knew he read them because he would recite a line to me if I asked for a favor. Over the years Dad had often remarked how I was the most even-keeled of his children. It never sat well with me that he preferred my presence simply because I had a passive demeanor. I felt the label discouraged me from speaking up when it was justified. To speak up meant to rock the boat, and to rock the boat meant going against all that he valued. And now he seemed to think his children had malicious intent behind our reactions to our parents' separation.

Dad was bearing witness to a whole new facet of my personality, and I must have lost his affection the moment I demonstrated he didn't have my unfailing support. That I could advocate for civility and compassion after what my mother did to him must have felt like yet another betrayal. But I couldn't play favorites anymore; seeing my parents together again as a unit was far more important to me. They were both needed to keep the family whole.

With his newly developed acid tongue, Dad spoke as though he were the one who had left my mother. "I'm glad it's over. Life is miserable with a spouse you can never please." To remind us that he was the only one looking after our needs, he announced, "Your mother is off diddling every Black man in town."

I struggled to navigate this new, unfamiliar territory in which cause and effect no longer seemed congruent. With the intention of preventing my parents' separation from devolving into a race issue, I purchased a T-shirt with the saying Love Sees No Color printed in rainbow lettering across the front. The spirit of the gesture was not received, however. Upon noticing my shirt, Dad scoffed incredulously and shook his head. Without saying a word, he turned and left the room. His silence revealed that he didn't view me as a confused but well-intentioned child caught in the war zone of her parents' separation. Instead, my T-shirt's message was the equivalent of me thumbing my nose at him. It likely took him back to his own days as an unhappy teenager. Once, when his straitlaced military father had had a guest over, Dad came down from his bedroom shirtless with the word "Fuck" scrawled across his chest in black marker.

My parents lacked the mental tenacity to handle such large-scale stressors as a separation following a cross-country move, and without support to handle the fallout, my siblings and I turned on our parents and, at times, each other. All we had was each other, but since we were all live wires, having internalized the fear and anger that characterized our parents' separation, we often found ourselves at odds depending on which parent we backed at any given time. Holding grudges, giving the silent treatment, and trading insults became a self-perpetuating cycle. Whether or not we wanted to play, we were pawns in a terrible game. Mom and Dad's new habit of oversharing private details resulted in me inappropriately taking up one's cause and arguing it with the other, not realizing it was neither my business nor my responsibility to do so. It became a messier endeavor than anticipated as I found myself continually switching sides, which affected my determination as to who had really been dealt the raw deal.

Growing up I had an unquestioning certainty that God had a grand plan for us all, the world and its inhabitants were inherently good, and good would always triumph over evil, when in reality this outlook was merely a luxury born of a stable childhood, in a sheltered environment, with a spiritual philosophy to guide us in all actions. The very peace of mind my parents had given me as a youngster had been snatched away with their separation, and for the first time I saw a real ugliness to life. I grew increasingly disillusioned, having been thrust into the sordid, harsh realities of adulthood. Although this was a progression I supposed all teenagers must undergo in the process of gaining a separate identity from their parents, it was deeply disturbing to no longer be able to view Mom and Dad as benevolent guardians but rather as emotionally volatile peers. It terrified me that two people who had appeared to be in a stable marriage, have a strong moral compass, and be dedicated to their children could so drastically change. This threw everything in the world into question for me. I no longer felt secure, and it appeared my siblings and I were going to have to fend for ourselves going forward.

I wondered at what point children whose parents didn't split up experienced an organic exit from childhood. I felt I was standing on the edge of an ever-widening chasm and wished more than anything to get back to the other side where I'd spent the first fourteen years of my life. I yearned to reclaim the safety I'd felt as a child, that deeply held belief that my parents knew best and had our best interests at heart. I wanted it to last forever.

Chapter 38

One evening I called my three younger siblings into the kitchen and told them that they needed to start pitching in around the house. I had drafted a list of chores assigned to each sibling. As I read off the items, Ben and Ryan started bickering with each other, and Heidi looked at me with a scowl on her face.

"Dad," I snapped, "can you back me up here?"

I looked at him sitting hunched over a plate of nachos at the table. The familiar cheesy, salty scent had become the smell of defeat in our house. This was all Dad made for dinner anymore, and they were just for him. He didn't even top them with beans or anything other than cheese. He paired them with salsa out of a jar. I'd certainly never seen nachos on the menu back in Vermont. If they had been, Dad would have made his own artisanal tortilla chips and salsa from scratch. But there he was, night after night, tucking into a plate of sad nachos, in his own world. It was like he wasn't even aware of our presence when we came into the kitchen to scrounge up some food for ourselves.

My father glanced up and raised his brows, as though completely unaware of the commotion around him.

"Ugh! Forget it!" I announced, tossing the chore chart onto the counter. *Dad is too preoccupied these days*, I thought, returning to my room. If he was home, he sought seclusion behind a closed door to play folk music on his guitar and practice tying sailing knots with a short length of rope.

Each weekday morning Dad would ask me, "Do you mind if I leave for work early?"

He was now serving as a teaching assistant at a preschool that his former colleague Maude had opened. This arrangement meant I would have to help my siblings get ready and ensure they walked to school on time. I wanted to see parental dedication from my father but didn't feel at liberty to prevent him from going to work, so I reluctantly consented.

"Okay! Bye!" Dad would say, darting out the door to his car. Despite his having always maintained a strong work ethic, I couldn't remember seeing him that eager in the mornings before.

Chapter 39

Visiting Mom for the first time at her new apartment, I immediately noticed that her hair had been restored to the bright golden hue it had been before she went through five pregnancies. She seemed effervescent.

A framed still life on the kitchen wall of a ceramic jug and two apples on a table also caught my eye. Though it was just a print inside a beige laminate frame, acquired along with a meager furniture selection from Goodwill, it gave me a great sense of peace to look at it. I didn't know how any kitchen could be complete without such a painting.

When Mom's eyes fell on Dad's ring adorning my thumb, she became visibly agitated.

"What are you doing with that?" she asked sharply.

"Dad gave it to me," I replied in a low voice.

"If he doesn't want it anymore," she said, "then it belongs to me."

I couldn't fathom why Mom would want the ring when she was the one who had ended the marriage. Regardless, I had no interest in fighting to keep it, especially when it hadn't felt right for the ring to be in my possession in the first place. I handed it over, with both relief and trepidation. Mom slipped off her own wedding band in order to secure my father's behind it. She would continue wearing the two together like that for another year or two, except when on a date.

Although I was fine with capitulating to Mom's wishes on this matter, I feared my father's disappointment, for just as quickly as she'd noticed me wearing his ring, I knew he'd notice its absence. Sure enough, upon my return to the Issaquah house, Dad questioned me immediately. When I meekly informed him that his ring was now in my mother's possession, he let out an exasperated sigh and slowly shook his head.

Chapter 40

In between classes one afternoon, I sat in the small common area on campus, reading. It was set up cafe-style, with round tables to encourage socializing. I sat alone, as usual. Two students were chatting nearby.

"She looks really young," I overheard one of the boys telling the other, as if it were unsettling to him.

"Hey, how old are you?" he called over to me.

"Fourteen," I said nervously. The boys appeared to be between seventeen and eighteen. I still didn't wear makeup or do anything to style my long brown hair other than pull it back in a ponytail, which only exacerbated my youthful appearance.

"You look really young ..." he repeated, trailing off. The astonishment on his face embarrassed me.

When the boys went back to talking amongst themselves, I returned to staring down at my book. Flooded with emotion, I merely pretended to read as I could no longer process the words.

I already felt like an outsider at the school, and the spotlight that this student had shone on my alien presence amongst these returning dropouts and unwed teen mothers was a wake-up call.

I'd been considering asking Mom if I could move in with her permanently. Her apartment was located in Bellevue, and since she worked in a health food store in the downtown area, it offered access to a mall, parks, and lakefront views.

Karina had been living with Mom for some time and had just graduated from the alternative high school that was a short walk down the street from the apartment complex. Off-Campus was an institution where there were no classes, just one-on-one sessions with teachers in their individual offices. I found this model appealing as it would enable me to avoid other teens, with whom I didn't seem to know how to relate anymore, and it would get me out of the misery of living in the Issaquah house. Karina loved her school and said she would help me get enrolled. The prospect felt increasingly compelling, even though it would require me to live with my mother, with whom I had a tenuous relationship at best. To live with her was to acknowledge the permanence of my parents' separation—since she was the one who had moved on. However, between an equally undesirable and unfulfilling living arrangement in the home of either parent, the lure of a class-free school won out for me.

Trying to decide which of my parents to live with reminded me of the time they had taken us to the drive-in to watch *Poltergeist* when we were far too young. Karina, Ben, and I wore our pajamas since we would be staying inside the van. I felt cozy in my flannel sleepwear, huddled together with my family. But with such scary things occurring on the screen, I was so frightened I blocked my ears and turned to watch a movie on the other side of the lot out the back window. The latter featured an unnecessarily long sex scene, with a couple canoodling on a bed in various stages of undress each time I looked from one screen to the other. I didn't know whether to continue trembling in terror while watching the horror film or feel I was doing something bad by watching the sex scene.

While my siblings also seemed resentful of our father's complete lack of concern, I doubted they took it as personally as I did. Given that I'd always enjoyed a close relationship with Dad, it felt like the worst sort of abandonment to have lost his affection. He had always loved me unconditionally, but now it was clearly conditional. I got the sense he didn't like me as a teenager.

Ultimately, I decided to join Mom. Her apartment—though just a one-bedroom—felt more like a home than the dark Issaquah house. At least I wouldn't be used for childcare anymore.

Chapter 41

As soon as school was out in June, I joined Karina at Mom's apartment at Whispering Pines. With two full-size mattresses atop box springs in the bedroom, Karina and I shared one, and when Heidi came to visit for extended periods of time, she shared with Mom. While the living arrangement was far from ideal, true to her word, my older sister took me to get enrolled for the fall at Off-Campus High School.

As I sat on the couch with Karina, Mom sat across from us and informed me about her new boyfriend, a man named Antoine whom she'd met at the gym. Still holding out hope for a reconciliation between my parents, I frowned at the unwelcome news.

What happened to her personal trainer? I wondered. Why such a quick transition away from the man for whom she'd thrown away her marriage?

She told us how any time she suggested they go back to his place, Antoine would say they couldn't because his roommate was home. She suspected Antoine had a wife.

"Even if he is married," she said, "he's too good not to be shared."

As she described Antoine's positive features, I stared at her hair, wondering whether it had taken bleach to lighten it that much.

Antoine came around often. He was a fit Black man with close-cropped hair and long eyelashes, who left a trail of cologne wherever he walked. He was friendly enough to my siblings and me, but in the slightly exaggerated fashion of someone maintaining decorum to impress his girlfriend.

Though Antoine never failed to appear in a silk shirt, dressy slacks, and patent leather shoes as if for a night on the town, he didn't take Mom out as often as they stayed in. When he arrived, they would disappear into the bedroom while my sisters and I sat in the living room watching TV.

How could a man possibly feel comfortable having sex with his girlfriend while her children were home? I wondered.

When Antoine was a medic in the Gulf War, every wounded soldier who came across his surgery table had to be photographed for record-keeping purposes. During one visit he put on a slide show in our living room of the close-ups he'd taken of missing limbs and gaping wounds. Shredded flesh, blood, and shrapnel were displayed in vivid color. It was gruesome, but I felt compelled to acknowledge the soldiers' extreme sacrifices. I was surprised to learn that even as a radiologist, Antoine had been required to carry an M16 rifle on him at all times. He said it had become like another appendage.

Chapter 42

Having moved twice and attended three different high schools, I'd lost touch with old friends and had none outside my siblings. I was over the moon upon receiving a call from Grant Preston, the senior from Newport High I'd met and developed a crush on while attending the same after-school club that focused on environmental protection. Since leaving Newport, I'd talked about Grant so often that Dad started referring to me as "Motor Mouth."

Like me, Grant was vegetarian, which I took as a sign that we were meant for each other. He parted his sandy blond hair off to one side, had blue eyes, and stood an inch shorter than me. It was his soft-spoken, laid-back demeanor that I found the most appealing. We chatted for a bit over the phone, catching up on all that I'd missed since moving away. Then he asked about my plans for the coming weekend.

"I'm not doing anything," I said, looking self-consciously over at the couch where Mom and Karina were sitting, overhearing every word. It was embarrassing to have them witness my vulnerability.

I had hung out with Grant only in group scenarios before and felt my pulse quicken to be invited solo to a laser music show in Seattle. After accepting and hanging up the phone, I jumped up and down.

"Oh my God, I'm so happy! I'm so happy!" I cried. "Grant's taking me on a date!" I clasped my hands under my chin and stared at Mom and Karina, who exchanged a glance with each other. They grinned back at me.

"It sounds like you have real feelings for this guy," my sister said.

As Friday neared, I found my anxiety about my first-ever date growing. Every time I thought about Grant, my stomach lurched. I started getting ready at five o'clock even though he wasn't picking me up until seven. I applied mascara and eyeliner and spritzed vanilla musk perfume on both wrists.

When Grant arrived at the door, I greeted him more bashfully than I would have preferred. He looked exactly as I remembered. Smiling at me sweetly, he gave me a quick hug. On the twenty-minute drive to Seattle, we discussed music preferences, his college plans, and our individual hopes for the future.

Reclining in our chairs inside the darkened theater, we looked up at the dome above as fog machines provided a backdrop for multicolored lights paired with U2 songs. The entire show I was preoccupied with whether Grant would try to hold my hand. When he didn't, I was both surprised and relieved. By the time he walked me to my doorstep at eleven o'clock that night, however, he had a determined look on his face.

"It was great getting to know you better," he whispered, standing close. One of his arms alighted on my lower back, and he tenderly kissed me. An embarrassing sound involuntarily escaped my lips, a low mewling that revealed I was but a child playing dress-up. I teetered a half step backward with a nervous laugh, glancing at the apartment door and willing it to open.

"Well, goodnight," I said.

Turning my key in the lock, I quickly ducked inside. As soon as the door was closed behind me, I collapsed my back against it. I had told myself before the date that if Grant kissed me, I wouldn't let anyone in my family know because they were sure to tease me. There was no avoiding it, however, as Karina was standing just a couple feet away staring at me.

"Oh my God, he kissed me!" I blurted, immediately betraying myself.

"I know!" my sister said, smiling and pointing at the peephole in the door. "I saw."

Mom, who was sitting on the couch, started firing questions at me about the date. Without another word, I dashed into the bathroom where I began scrubbing my mouth vigorously with hot water and soap. I didn't know why

I felt compelled to do such a thing. Grant had been a perfect gentleman, not using tongue or pulling any other funny business. But it was all so foreign.

I exited the bathroom to the sound of Mom and Karina snickering. My sister was still standing in the same spot.

"You're such a chicken, Angie," she said.

Lacking a retort, I shrugged and smiled sheepishly. In the bedroom, I wrote in my diary how it felt like my consciousness left my body while the whole scene on the doorstep played out. I hadn't experienced any sensation other than that of butterflies in my stomach. I couldn't say how long our goodbye had lasted; it might have been five seconds or five minutes.

I didn't have the confidence to tell Grant I wasn't ready for a relationship. While I felt bad he might take my silence as rejection, he didn't call me again either. Perhaps he had sensed I was in over my head. Forever afterward I associated the vanilla musk fragrance with being kissed, and I never wore it again since catching so much as a whiff made me queasy.

Recognizing that I wasn't ready to start dating after all, I feared something was wrong with me, judging by Mom's hypersexuality and the fact that Karina had started dating at fifteen. I figured the best thing for me to do was conduct private research on my own terms. I expressed my desire to look at a *Playgirl* magazine, which caused Mom to burst into laughter.

"Oh!" she exclaimed with delight. "Antoine is coming over tonight, and I'll ask him to stop by a store on his way to pick one up for you!" It clearly amused her to make this unconventional request of him.

It was strange to think about how just four years prior, Mom had confiscated a *Mad* magazine from me, claiming it wasn't appropriate reading material for my age, and had also forbidden me to watch *Dirty Dancing* with my friends when I was twelve.

When Antoine arrived, he pulled the magazine out of a paper bag and handed it to me with a smirk. It was wrapped in plastic, making it seem highly taboo. Only after he and Mom had disappeared into the bedroom with a bottle of wine did I remove the wrapping as I sat on the couch. A minute later I froze upon noticing Antoine peeking at me from around the corner. I hoped from his perspective the situation was merely amusing and not titillating. The situation felt awfully lascivious since I didn't have anywhere to go for privacy in the one-bedroom apartment other than the bathroom if it came to it. Having been caught, Antoine smiled and returned to the bedroom, leaving me to wonder how long he would have lingered had I not spotted him.

With both of my sisters elsewhere, I sat in the stillness of the living room observing the cover model's bare chest and flowing sandy blond locks, taking the time to read every line of text. Hesitant to open the magazine, I told myself I could still back out; I could throw it away and pretend none of this had ever happened. However, curiosity got the best of me, and I turned the page.

Oh ... my ... God. This is what women are supposed to find attractive? I thought. The cover model's spread featured photographs of him engaged in various activities while mysteriously in a state of arousal. In one he sat on his living room floor, back against the couch, reading literature, with his erection draped over his thigh.

Mom came out in a bathrobe to grab a corkscrew and wine glasses from the kitchen. Given that she had gotten married before reaching the legal drinking age and had been of a faith that discouraged the consumption of alcohol, it was surreal seeing her enjoy wine for the first time at thirty-five. She perched on the arm of the couch to look over my shoulder.

"Oh, that's interesting," she said of one model. "He's uncircumcised."

"How can you tell?" I asked, looking up at her.

"Because of that skin there," she said, pressing her finger against the tip of the model's penis. All I saw were his private parts on graphic display, the same as every other man throughout the glossy pages. Mom returned to the bedroom, closing the door behind her. I disposed of the magazine now that my curiosity had been satiated. My mind was made up: I was never going to go near a man's ding-a-ling.

Chapter 43

For periods of time life was good, and we all got along. Karina and I tested boundaries by asking Mom to purchase wine coolers for us, which she did, and we pretended to enjoy the taste as we sipped them in the living room. Mom would take us rollerblading along the waterfront like we were normal people. But we all still had raw, volatile emotions, and it took very little for any one of us to get upset and give the others the silent treatment.

I couldn't seem to get along with Mom for any great length of time, being fundamentally at odds with her lifestyle. I didn't want her as a friend; I wanted her to be a real mother. The kind that provided unconditional support, reassuring hugs, and set boundaries to show she cared about my safety.

Whenever Karina and Mom were getting along, they were the best of friends and of like minds. They thought me self-righteous, and if I said something that struck them as judgmental or naive, they accused me of being a daddy's girl, called me a prude, or referred to me as the "holy one" in the family. When they were at odds, I was forced to choose whether to align with Mom or my sister, and both gave me a hard time for being friends with the other.

During one such period when Karina was giving Mom the cold shoulder, she returned home from work and noticed the rollerblades Mom had bought me that afternoon.

"Well," she said snidely, "I guess kissing Mom's butt lately has paid off."

"I haven't been kissing Mom's butt," I protested. "We've just been getting along." Even as the words left my mouth, I was flooded with doubt. Perhaps Mom had in fact bought my allegiance.

One weekend afternoon, as I napped in the bedroom and Karina and Heidi watched TV in the living room, Mom and Antoine—with nowhere else to go—were kissing in the bathroom. I don't know what possessed them to leave the door open, but when Karina caught them, she flew into a rage. I heard her call Mom a bitch just before she barged into the bedroom and began packing.

I watched as my sister stuffed clothes into a backpack while rebuffing Mom's attempts to calm her down. Karina then stormed out of the apartment without a word to anyone. She called me later to let me know that she'd arranged to move into a friend's spare bedroom, a half hour's drive south of Mom's apartment, which meant I wouldn't get to see her very often.

"It's probably the only way she could have left home," Mom mused. "By being mad at me."

As much as I agreed with Karina that Mom's actions were unacceptable, I couldn't believe she'd called the woman who birthed her that terrible word.

Chapter 44

After realizing she wasn't going to shake her kids off, Mom upgraded to a two-bedroom apartment in the same complex. A freshly renovated corner unit on the top floor, right off the stairway, it was downright luxurious. Every wall, door, and ceiling was pristine white, and our feet were the first to walk upon the light-gray carpeting that extended the length of the unit from the living room to the bedrooms, which faced out onto the parking lot. It was the nicest home any of us had been in since leaving Vermont, which seemed to indicate the start of a better life.

Having become enamored of Native American traditions, Mom pinned a dream catcher over her bed and carried a smoldering sage smudge stick around the apartment to cleanse it of bad spirits.

Karina moved back in, and we shared a full-size bed in one room, while Heidi slept in a twin-size bed in Mom's room. With Ryan occasionally staying on the pull-out loveseat in the living room, the apartment looked less like a home than mattresses adrift at sea.

By switching to Off-Campus High School, I didn't meet others my age. The only exception was keyboarding class, where each student was assigned his or her own computer. But there was no socializing there either since the practice was timed. I'd registered for the course thinking it was a chance to learn how to play an instrument. By the time I realized it was actually a touch-typing class, I figured it would at the very least be an easy way to earn a good grade since I had used a typewriter before.

Being on campus for only two to three hours a day meant I had a lot of free time on my hands. I wouldn't bother getting up before ten o'clock in the morning, at which point I'd have a leisurely breakfast of toast and cereal, then walk down the street to meet with my teachers.

Early in the morning as she was getting ready, Mom sometimes opened my door and rummaged around in the closet that I shared with Karina. My sister, having already left for the day, always did so quietly so as not to wake me.

"Mom!" I'd groan into my pillow. "Why are you bothering me?" I'd have been up late the night prior, watching reruns or reading in bed with a flashlight.

"I need to borrow your jean jacket," she would say.

It didn't make any sense for her to pilfer from our wardrobe. We didn't wile away our weekends at the mall shopping as other teen girls might, and neither of us owned the kinds of colorful, flashy clothing Mom preferred. Karina wore basic denim with black T-shirts featuring a variety of Native American scenes and wolves howling at the moon, and my modest style—acquired at Goodwill—was now comprised of oversized drab pieces designed not to draw attention to myself. I wondered if the real reason Mom interrupted my sleep was that since she had to get up early to earn money, she wasn't about to have any freeloaders under her roof getting the luxury of sleeping in.

Chapter 45

Aside from the times I was tasked with babysitting younger siblings, I could have been out doing anything I wanted. With no curfew imposed upon me, I could have run with the worst kids and stayed out all night if I'd been so inclined. Yet I felt paralyzed by the amount of freedom I had. The world outside our door might as well have been the gaping maw of space, a great expanse of options, each with potentially dangerous consequences. The lack of structure and boundaries felt suffocating, and as any shred of confidence I may have once had dried up, I became increasingly withdrawn.

Sometimes during the day, I would sit on my bed and cry. I envisioned screaming at the four bare white walls that both protected and entrapped me, but I couldn't risk us being evicted. Our apartment was directly over the rental office, and the manager would surely resent sounds that would be off-putting to prospective tenants.

I had never before in my life spent so much time in bed while the sun was up, except for times when I was sick. It was a revelation how comforting it was—why hadn't I lounged in bed during the day before? Being on the island of my mattress reset all my emotional meters back to zero. It felt indulgent to be ensconced in the softness of the sheets under the comforting weight of the duvet, with the pliable pillows cradling my head. Of course, it ended with me taking a nap every afternoon. Reminded of the safety and comfort I felt each night at bedtime when I used to get tucked in with a kiss on the cheek as my parents made the rounds, it also called to mind a day when I partook of one of my favorite childhood pastimes.

Kneeling on the burgundy carpet in the family den, which used to be Mom and Dad's bedroom before the extension was completed on the house, I had flipped through records in a milk crate stored next to Dad's guitar case.

Locating my favorite album, Mississippi John Hurt's blues, I carried it to the vintage record player cabinet with carpeted speakers on either end. It was nearly the size of a dresser. I had to stand on tiptoe to draw up the lid and access the turntable inside. I gently slipped the disc out of its sleeve and placed it on the spinner. At five years old, I knew exactly how to set the needle without scratching the vinyl.

Lying on the floor with a pillow next to one of the speakers, I listened to the songs intently. A gentle, gritty voice told me about the hard life of a sharecropper in the South and how he'd had trouble all his days and found love in the midst of it. Rubbing the soft flannel pillowcase against my cheek as I sucked my thumb, I dropped off to sleep.

Upon awaking, I could tell a lot of time had passed since the record stopped. The door had been closed to ensure my nap went uninterrupted. Approaching the door, I'd intended to go find Dad, but stopped in my tracks upon hearing unfamiliar voices. I peered out to see Dad's brother Eldon and Mom's brother Dale standing in the kitchen talking to my father. I ran to Dad, who scooped me up. Wrapping my arms around his neck, I kept my gaze over his shoulder to avoid making eye contact with the unexpected visitors. My uncles chuckled. Dad gave me a reassuring hug, and I felt safe.

Chapter 46

For my fifteenth birthday, I asked for a periwinkle-blue phone I'd seen at Sears. It had a sleek, modern look, with oversized square buttons. Its youthful vibrancy promised I would have friends to call on it. After Mom bought it for me, I plugged it into my bedroom wall with anticipation. It was, unfortunately, on the same line as the kitchen phone, but it felt exhilarating to see it on my dresser nonetheless.

In the days that followed, I often found the phone missing from my room. It was inevitably discovered plugged in near Mom's bed. When I demanded an answer as to why she kept taking it, she shrugged it off.

"Antoine likes to call me late at night," she said, "so it's helpful to have a phone close by. You know, so it doesn't disturb you girls."

"But it's my phone," I implored, "and I want it to stay in my room."

"Oh, Angie," Mom said playfully, "no one calls for you anyway."

Even after being admonished, she started taking the phone from right under my watchful gaze. She would come into my room in the evening with a mischievous smile on her face, unplug the phone from the wall, and carry it back to her room without so much as a word as I glared at her. Each morning I would take the phone back, just to have the process repeated that evening. As annoying as this cycle was, the one benefit was no longer being subjected to Mom's sultry conversations on the kitchen phone, where I'd once overheard her enticing Antoine to come over by murmuring, "When will you grace me with your presence?" Sometimes the calls were with her sister though.

"Gloria says the best place to meet a man is at Alcoholics Anonymous meetings," Mom announced to Karina and me after one such conversation, like it was breaking news. "Their worst is behind them, so you don't have to work as hard to improve them."

Chapter 47

Since Karina had an after-school job and often hung out late with friends, I would have been unbearably lonely if I hadn't had my rat, Teddy, for company. I found a few ways to keep myself occupied and distracted from the loneliness. I watched Sally Jessy Raphael's daytime talk show, and in the evenings, after Mom and whichever of my siblings was living with us had gone to bed, I'd stay up watching reruns of *Night Court* and *Perfect Strangers*.

The most peaceful respite to be found on a sunny day was at the local cemetery. Just one block from our apartment, an expansive impeccably maintained cemetery was situated on an upward-sloping lawn that crested at a plateau, offering an incredible view of the Seattle skyline in the distance. The rows of marble gravestones were like a line of headboards indicating where each person was tucked snugly into bed. What was to become of me, I didn't know; but those laid to rest there already had their answers.

First, I would stop at the market across the street to purchase coconut cookies, sold loose in a big plastic bin. At two for a dollar, they were a treat I could afford with a handful of saved change. Cookies in hand, I would then head back across the street for a picnic of sorts. Surrounded by the silence and stillness of the tombstones, I would relax on a bench, contentedly nibbling away at my sweet, crunchy treats while basking in the sun and taking in the view.

When I started getting frequent stomachaches, I half-joked to Heidi about my suspicion that Mom was lacing my food with arsenic. However, the scenario from V.C. Andrews's *Flowers in the Attic* being carried out against me was unlikely. Mom was rarely present when I took my meals. Also, why would she poison her babysitter?

Checking out stacks of *Travel & Leisure* magazines from the library to slowly page through at home, I yearned to travel to any one of the featured locations where the classically beautiful models appeared carefree.

Due to Mom's insistence that I be present any time she wasn't there to care for Ryan, I felt imprisoned in the apartment. My parents played hot potato with my eight-year-old brother, neither of them wanting the burden of having him full-time, when the reality was he spent most of his waking hours at friends' houses outside of school.

As little affection as I had for Ryan, it felt awful to witness Mom force him out of the apartment. Choking back tears as his head hung low, he looked utterly dejected when he heard impatient honking from the parking lot, alerting him to my father's arrival. On one such occasion, I watched out my bedroom window, which faced the parking lot, as Dad waited in his coworker Maude's SUV. I had a clear view directly into the driver's side window and observed my father gripping the steering wheel with both hands. He wore his usual driving cap and oversized senior-citizen sunglasses. As my brother climbed into the back seat, weeping, I could tell that Dad didn't even address him. He didn't turn his head to acknowledge his child, and his mouth never moved. He barely waited until the door was closed before gunning it out of the parking lot.

I imagined it was a blow to my father's ego that his children preferred living with the woman who had scorned him, and yet they were still thrust back upon him.

Though I complained about my enforced role as babysitter, in truth I was finding myself becoming increasingly anxious about leaving the apartment. Mom's recklessness terrified me. I still craved structure and stability. Afraid even to go to the grocery store across the street alone when Mom sent me to fetch a gallon of milk, I would coerce a younger sibling to accompany me.

Likewise, my ten-minute walk to and from school was a struggle, knowing I'd be walking down a busy main street like a lone actor on stage before an enormous audience. *Those people are mocking me*, I would think as I passed the gas station and overheard two people laughing. *They're talking about how homely I am.* I walked fast so passersby wouldn't have as much time to scrutinize me. Even in warm weather I wore an oversized drab-olive army coat I'd bought at a military surplus store, feeling it offered some protection from judgmental eyes.

To my horror, I began developing an hourglass figure. I wore oversized shirts, attempting to hide the biological transformation that, even as a late bloomer, was happening faster than I was mentally prepared for.

Mom insisted that sports bras would give me the best support. Between the bulkiness of my large shirts and the pancaking effect of the bra, what I appreciated most was that it actually helped hide the existence of my breasts.

I kept a bra on at all times, even while sleeping. I gave serious consideration to leaving it on in the shower as well, with the added benefit of washing my laundry at the same time. Even still, I felt betrayed by my body and felt it was sending the wrong signal to men.

Once, two men had whistled at me from across the street. I was wearing denim shorts that I'd been concerned might be too high cut. The unwanted attention confirmed my fears. I felt at once flattered and disgusted at the concept of someone finding me attractive without even knowing me or caring about me as a person. Even worse was the teasing I would get at home.

"Where'd you get those big boobs from, Ang?" Karina would say, grinning while looking from Mom to me.

"Yeah, where did you get those from?" Mom would chime in. Then the two of them would cackle like hyenas.

"Men are gonna love you," Karina would say.

Uncomfortable with the implications of having an hourglass shape and fearful of encouraging more teasing if they sensed weakness, I would pretend like I was in on the joke.

"I must've gotten them from Dad's side of the family," I would say wryly. Since Dad only had brothers and we had never known his mother, it was anyone's guess what feminine traits could have been inherited from his side.

Karina and I had accompanied Mom to a gym once to try out the stationary bikes and treadmills, but I found the meat-market vibe intolerable. The room was lined with mirrors, and as my mother lifted weights, I could see men unabashedly ogling her as they engaged in their own workouts. I felt disgusted by the behavior, and although I didn't catch any men looking at me, I couldn't bear the possibility that they might. My self-consciousness prevented me from returning to the gym again.

I was certain that every man only wanted one thing from a woman and would do anything to get it. Thus, my regular outfit was a full-coverage T-shirt, my army jacket, and jeans. I refused to wear dresses or skirts.

As much as Mom seemed to resent being a mother, she was still a hugger. What should have been a pleasant, even comforting exchange had become off-putting. I couldn't help feeling repulsed, knowing she'd been in the arms of men who weren't my father.

Whenever Mom hugged me, she would immediately launch into teasing mode as soon as she pulled away. "What's this new way of hugging you're doing, Ang?" she would ask, and laugh. Then Karina would get in on the action and tease me about it as well. I would proclaim that nothing was unusual about the way I hugged, when in fact I was consciously caving forward so that just my shoulders touched the other person with no chance of contact in the chest zone.

Chapter 48

"Mom," I called, knocking on the door. "I need to use the bathroom!"
"I'd like some privacy please." She sounded annoyed.

"Can't you just wait outside a minute while I go?" I suggested, my voice rising an octave.

"Just come in," she said flatly.

I entered the narrow bathroom to find my mother sitting on the edge of the tub shaving what ought to have been her *private* region. Her legs splayed open, with one foot propped up to the side. She was nude, save for a pink satin robe left unsashed. The silky lapels hung limply at her sides, and her breasts hung at eye level as I sat on the toilet to urinate.

"Well, this isn't awkward at all," I muttered sarcastically, averting my gaze.

"Don't look if it bothers you so much," Mom said.

Across from me a collection of sheer teddies and thongs were hanging to dry on the towel rack, the sorts of things never seen in our house in Vermont back when Mom used to leave the hair wherever it grew, including her armpits.

"New lingerie?" I asked wryly.

"Mind your business," Mom said.

The array of intimate wear, which she regularly hand-washed and line-dried, was my introduction to the concept of "date" panties. Up until that point I'd been under the impression that all underwear came in packs of three, were made of pastel-colored cotton, and were strictly for comfort beneath one's clothing.

"I'm going out with Antoine tonight, so I want you to take care of Ryan."

"Again?" I said, flushing the toilet. "You never even spend time with us."

"Any time a parent is present in the house, whether they're in the same room as the children or not, counts as quality time."

Mom never raised her voice with us. Instead, she wielded the icy blade of conviction. With her sense that she was right in all demands and decrees, she granted herself unquestionable authority, negating the need to shout in order to bend others to her will.

"Well, what if I already had plans?"

"I'm not in the mood for back talk, Angie," she said. "I just need you to be here for Ryan. You know he won't be around anyway; he's probably at CJ's."

"Whether or not he's physically here is beside the point," I said, washing my hands. "It still requires me to sit at home. For nothing."

Mom sighed and stopped mid-shave. She gave me a hard look.

"I said I'm not in the mood for back talk. I expect you to do as I say and watch your brother while I'm out."

"You never even ask me first," I said, shaking my hands over the sink while looking around for a towel.

"We both know you don't have plans," she said, resuming her task with the razor. "And you can follow my rules or choose not to live under my roof."

"That's a real nice thing to say to your fifteen-year-old daughter," I grumbled. Unable to locate a towel, I resorted to wiping my hands on my jeans.

Glancing in the mirror at my plain face, I saw my father's brown eyes looking back at me. They were too narrow relative to my broad forehead and round face. I had an odd combination of my parents' noses, as if the slightly bulbous tip of Mom's had been jammed onto the end of Dad's. The best thing I could say about myself was that I had a clear complexion, uncharacteristic of teenagers.

Since Mom had upgraded to a two-bedroom apartment, I was glad Karina and I no longer had to share a room with her. Happy to take advantage of my own space, I closed my bedroom door behind me.

"Teddy," I cooed, bending over my pet rat's cage. "Ready to come out for a visit?" I lowered my cupped hand, palm side up. He hopped on with his soft pink paws resting on my wrist, and I lifted him out of the glass tank. I set him on the carpet, and he scampered off.

Keeping Teddy confined to a cage was the last thing I wanted to do, so whenever I was in my room, I let him have free rein. But I also had to protect him from the things that could hurt him. Once, he chewed a hole through a bottle of glue. The sticky white substance coated his nose and leaked onto the carpet. It was stressful work ensuring no residue was left behind on his fur as I gently cleaned his face with a moistened washcloth.

My favorite sound was the scrabbling from the side of the bed as Teddy climbed up the comforter. He employed unbelievable strength and dexterity to claw his way up to visit me. My rat was handsome, with golden fur, black eyes, and a long pink tail. Intelligent too—he nearly always came to me when I called him. When he didn't, I knew it meant he was inside the bed's box spring, which he had accessed by tearing a hole in the gauzy sheet stapled to the bottom. I especially loved it when he tickled my chin with his soft nose and whiskers, his version of a kiss. He did a great job of keeping me company, especially since he'd adapted to my schedule, equally happy to visit during the day or night.

In one particular instance, I had a few pieces of popcorn for Teddy on my bedside table and offered him one. He took it gently with his mouth, sat upright on the bed to grasp the snack between both paws, and commenced nibbling.

Sometime later the door opened. Mom leaned in, bright as a rainbow between her makeup and silk harlequin jacket over a red velvet dress.

"Is it overkill for me to wear this necklace with these earrings?" she asked of her costume jewelry.

"I read in *Seventeen* magazine that you shouldn't pair a flashy necklace with big earrings," I said. "It ends up looking gaudy. You'll have to choose between them."

"Okay, that's a good tip," she said cheerfully. "Thank you, sweetheart." She withdrew, closing the door.

I alternated between reading *A Cat of a Different Color*, a Lydia Adamson mystery for cat lovers, and feeding Teddy the rest of the popcorn whenever he came scampering back for more.

When Mom entered again, sans necklace, she approached my bedside smiling at us. At first, she had been squeamish around Teddy. However, he soon won her over with his lovable demeanor, and she would even stroke his fur occasionally. "Are you two going to stay up all night reading?"

"Yup."

"Okay," Mom said, leaning down to kiss me. "Don't forget to listen for your brother's knock."

Chapter 49

I was in the process of frying up a package of soy hot dogs when there was a rapid pounding on the front door. I opened it to find Ryan with a scowl on his face darker than any eight-year-old should have had. I stepped aside to let him pass, and he entered without greeting me. He kicked off his sneakers and went into the living room. I could hear the TV turn on.

"Have you been playing with CJ?" I called, as I returned to my task in the kitchen.

"Yup," Ryan said grumpily. "But we got into a fight over video games."

"Well, dinner will be ready shortly," I said.

My mother was in her bedroom with her sole female friend, a divorced woman she occasionally partnered with at the gym. Deandra was rather birdlike—tall and thin, with a sizable beak of a nose. She wore too much foundation on her face, creating a distinct color differentiation immediately below her chin, and kept her curly brown hair in a youthful bob.

"We're going to watch a film," Mom had said, as she and Deandra headed to her room and closed the door. I imagined they would be watching something boring about bodybuilding on her small television set with a built-in VCR.

"Dinner's ready," I called out, loud enough for Mom to hear, as I placed ketchup, mustard, and hot dog buns on the counter.

Ryan came into the kitchen, assembled two hot dogs which he doused with ketchup, and took them back to the living room to eat while watching his favorite TV show, *Kung Fu: The Legend Continues.*

A couple of minutes later Mom and Deandra came into the kitchen. Each grasped a single soy hot dog in her bare hand, holding it upright from one end like a torch. They looked as eager as children with lollypops. Silently retreating back to my mother's room, the door closed once again.

I froze, staring in confusion at the untouched condiments and buns on the counter. I knew then that the two women weren't watching something educational like bodybuilding best practices or wholesome like *Howards End*. More likely, it was a training video about how to please your man.

What were the odds of me serving a phallic dinner the very same evening they planned to watch porn? As much as I didn't want to imagine what they were doing, it was clear my dinner had become a prop for whatever X-rated activity they were engaged in.

Chapter 50

The next evening Mom didn't eat what I had prepared for dinner, instead informing me she had last-minute plans to go out with a man from Ghana that she had met at her health food store.

"Why didn't you do the laundry today like I asked you to?" she scolded.

I followed her into her bedroom where she selected a dress from the walk-in closet. "I didn't get around to it," I said, "but I did cook dinner and vacuum the apartment."

"I've been working all day to keep a roof over our heads," she said, "and you can't even lift a finger to help out."

"I just said I cooked and vacuumed," I responded, though I felt ashamed for not having taken the additional effort to go to the laundry room across the complex.

"Yeah, well I needed the laundry done so that I'd have clothes to wear to work tomorrow." Her tone was heavy with disappointment.

I thought about how my mother took time to select her outfit for work each morning, carefully coordinating each piece. She ironed her clothes every single day, from the jeans purchased at discount department stores to the one-off blouse that looked like it could have once passed for fashionable. Forced to modernize with a severely limited budget, she had cobbled together a small collection of economically priced pieces. They were certainly more feminine and closer to being in style than anything she'd worn back in Vermont but fell short of the silk blouses, pantsuits, high heels, and name brand purses sported by other women in the downtown Bellevue area where my mother's health food store was located.

While ironing, Mom occasionally let a whooshing sigh escape her lips. An unconscious habit, it was a sound that made me feel sad. It revealed an underlying existence of hopes and dreams not met by her current circumstances.

"I need you to babysit your brother tonight," Mom said, holding up different jackets against the pink dress she had selected.

"I hate being stuck here," I said, "especially since Ryan probably won't even be here all night."

"Where is your brother now?" she asked, opening her lingerie drawer.

"I don't know," I said dismissively. "He never came home after school, so I assume he's down at CJ's."

"Well, you have to be here in case he comes home," she said, beginning to strip off her work clothes.

"Fine," I sighed, averting my gaze.

When her date arrived, Mom answered the door as enthusiastically as a debutante welcoming esteemed guests to her gala. She led him into the living room, where I was sitting.

"Ayodelé, this is my daughter Angie," she said, gesturing in my direction.

He was a stout, dark-skinned man with dense, bushy hair, wearing an ornately embroidered dark tunic over black slacks. He didn't look like the men Mom had previously shown interest in, the muscular fitness addicts with neatly trimmed hair and flashy wardrobes who left traces of musky cologne on my hand when we were introduced.

"It is very nice to meet you," he said, with a thick accent.

"It's nice to meet you too," I said, smiling. Although I didn't have anything against him personally, the obligatory song and dance was vexing, and I was annoyed with my mother's insistence that I meet every man who came through our door.

"Well, we're off," Mom said in a singsong manner as she leaned down to kiss my cheek. "I love you, sweetheart."

Chapter 51

When I was in tenth grade, my mother's parents came to visit from North Carolina. Mom drove us kids over to see them at Aunt Gloria's house. It had been several years since we last saw them in Vermont. Though I loved my grandparents, it wasn't good timing because I knew I couldn't pretend everything was fine at home.

As the story went, my grandparents weren't fond of Dad back when he had impregnated their teenaged daughter. However, he'd grown on them over the years, and they were none too pleased with Mom for having left him.

Acknowledging the sadness in our eyes, I suppose, my grandmother laid into Mom for the injustice she'd done to her children. I'd never heard her sound like anything other than a sweet grandmother. She had a gray bob, wore large glasses, and had on a denim dress over a T-shirt. She spoke with a Southern accent.

When Mom attempted to interject, Grandma cut her off.

"You apparently won't learn until it's too late and one of your children is dead."

While her delivery was unnecessarily melodramatic, I appreciated that someone was on our side and willing to take my mother to task. When I was younger, the thought of my parents dying had always made my eyes well up with tears. Did Mom and Dad not consider the fragility of life in this same way?

"I'm not going to stand here and take this," Mom said. "I hope you enjoy your visit. Come on, kids!"

Karina, Ben, Heidi, and I fell in line obediently, following her out of Gloria's house.

"I'm staying here," Ryan announced, holding his ground in my aunt's living room. His unkempt auburn curls looked like wildfire licking across the dry plains.

"You're coming with me," Mom said firmly, turning to look at him through the doorway. He stared at Mom defiantly with his dark, beady eyes. Karina, Ben, Heidi, and I watched silently.

"Ryan told me things are bad at home," Gloria said, blocking the threshold with her body. "I'm letting him stay here as long as he wants." She and Mom locked eyes for a tense moment.

"Come on, kids!" Mom demanded.

Ben, Heidi, and I crammed into the back seat of the tiny hatchback, cowering together while Karina was stuck sitting up front.

"Why didn't you kids defend me?" Mom snapped, glaring at us through the rearview mirror. "My mother rips me apart, and my own children stand by not saying a goddamn word in my defense." She shook her head.

You're a selfish mother, and everything Grandma said was right, I thought. But I couldn't say that out loud. None of us offered a response, and it was a silent ride home.

Chapter 52

My grandmother's warning to Mom was prescient. I had been fantasizing regularly about stepping in front of a speeding fire truck. It comforted me to think I could check out at any time. Most of all, I delighted in imagining how, when a police officer came to inform Mom that her fifteen-year-old daughter had been crushed by a fire truck, she would know it was personal.

Mom's new boyfriend, Dez, was a firefighter. Prior to meeting him, she had never mentioned an interest in becoming a firefighter. Yet while dating him, she wouldn't stop talking about how it was the natural next step for her, still being in her prime since the bodybuilding competition.

I was beginning to see a pattern. Mom picked up the traits of whomever she spent the most time with. That meant Vermont Mom was just a chameleon of Dad, and in Washington she adapted to her suitors. When she fancied the next person, she simply traded interests.

Mom acted like it had been her lifelong dream to be a firefighter and started taking steps to prepare. In addition to being required to demonstrate that she could carry a heavy fire hose on her shoulder while running up several flights of stairs, she also had to pass a lengthy exam. It struck me as irresponsible for a mother of five to welcome a job that would involve regularly risking her life, and I was relieved when she failed the exam. She said it was the math section that had stumped her.

Although I refrained from informing my school counselor Renee that I was suicidal, what I did share in our sessions was enough for her to arrange a psychological evaluation for me at a nearby mental health facility. Since Mom was unavailable at the scheduled time, I was forced to ask Dad to give me a ride to the appointment, a favor I was loathe to request. He didn't inquire why I had been scheduled for the evaluation. It was an awkward trip there and back with nothing said along the way other than me providing directions and Dad saying he would wait in the car. He avoided making eye contact with me. Because he had refused marriage counseling with Mom, I was under the impression he thought a person weak for seeking therapy.

The psychologist softly asked me a series of questions, such as whether I'd ever heard voices talking directly to me from the TV or radio. I felt embarrassed at first, then smug when I imagined how being locked away in a mental ward would show my parents. I was both relieved and disappointed when at the end of the session I was given a clean bill of health, leaving the building feeling as though it had been a waste of time. Worse than anything was that my appointment hadn't elicited the slightest concern from either parent.

My counselor was an incredibly compassionate woman. Having served as Karina's counselor before me, Renee was already familiar with what was going on in my home before I started seeing her regularly. She had close-cropped, curly silver hair and a ready smile. I appreciated that she listened attentively and always remembered everything I told her. She made me feel as though my viewpoint and struggles were valid, and continually encouraged me to look out for myself. Renee's most common refrain during our sessions was, "If the ship is sinking, you have to get off the ship."

"But what about my siblings?" I would ask. "I can't just leave them behind."

"There is nothing you can do for them," she would say gently. "All you can do is lead by example. When they see you making smart choices for yourself, they will emulate you."

Renee's suggestion certainly seemed to make sense, but it was a frightening proposition. I had in fact fantasized about running away from home and joining the growing number of squatters in Seattle. I had seen news coverage of the homeless youth that resided in abandoned buildings in the city. Knowing that neglected children often joined gangs for a sense of family, I imagined I would find camaraderie with the squatters.

Ultimately, I realized that that living situation would never work for me because I required a clean bed, a real bathroom, regular meals, and an assurance of physical safety. Further, I had an inner drive to do right by myself by finishing high school.

With so few options, I felt torn, as I wasn't in a healthy environment in Mom's apartment. I'd had a nightmare in which my mother's beau du jour had designs on me. It wasn't anyone I'd met in real life; I just knew in the dream that he was her boyfriend. The man and I were both sitting on my mother's bed, and I was trying to inch away as he continued advancing toward me. My mother was standing in the room, but with her back to us. I was terrified and yearned for her to protect me, but she refused to turn around, even as the man made it clear that he would go through with this vile act. Fortunately, I'd awoken before the nightmare turned graphic, but not before I felt betrayed by my mother.

Chapter 53

On the evening that Mom intended to bring her fifth suitor, Winston, home, I told her I had no intention of meeting him.

"Oh yes you will!" she demanded.

"Then I won't be polite!" I said.

"Oh yes you will!"

I insisted that I was no longer going to acknowledge the parade of men coming in through our front door or stand for this kind of treatment. For the first time, I felt angry enough that it gave me the courage to tell her off. I wanted to lay into her and make her feel my pain, when I suddenly paused and realized I could play this to my advantage. I decided to go in a different direction.

"All right," I said calmly. "I'll be nice to your date. If you pay me twenty dollars."

My mother looked me square in the eye for a moment, perhaps contemplating whether to call my bluff. "Okay," she said, equally calmly. I stared after her in surprise as she fetched her purse. She set a twenty into my palm, which I accepted silently, still amazed that my unplanned ultimatum had worked. I was also taken aback that she actually had that much in her wallet. I almost felt guilty taking what was likely all she had left to her name. However, I assuaged my guilt with the knowledge that Mom's date would pay her way all evening.

The real problem was feeling as dirty as a prostitute for accepting money to be civil to a stranger. Yet I couldn't help imagining all the things I could do with so much money. I was already planning ahead to the iced latte I would get from the espresso stand next door and a chocolate bar from the convenience store. Cash passed through my hands infrequently, as I didn't receive an allowance or payment for all the babysitting I did at home. This was a victory to be cherished.

When her date came knocking, Mom invited him inside. "Winston, this is my daughter Angie and my son Ryan," she said proudly, with an exaggerated sweep of her hand as if presenting a royal guest of honor. Ryan, who had returned from Aunt Gloria's house after deciding he missed Mom, was seated next to me on the couch watching TV. My little brother looked up just long enough to offer a disinterested greeting, but I stood to shake Winston's hand and smiled in a welcoming fashion.

"Nice to meet you kids," Winston said, with sincerity and a hint of a Southern accent. He wore a gray suit, a black silky undershirt, and a gold-toned watch. A scar shaped like a railroad track ran from the upper jaw of his left cheek to the edge of his mouth. I wondered how he'd gotten it.

Though relatively lean, Winston wasn't from Mom's gym. She had already told me that they'd met at a dance club in the local Red Lion Inn. He seemed like a nice man, but I wasn't counting on seeing him again as he looked a little older and less image-conscious than Mom's usual dates.

My mother kissed my cheek while I kept right on smiling as I stood with my hands clasped before me. "Well, we're off to the dance club," she said. "Don't wait up!"

As I sat back down on the couch, I thought about the cash I had just earned from my winning performance. I didn't know why my mother was insistent on introducing her men to us. She could have saved herself twenty dollars by simply not inviting the latest inside. Though worried I'd jeopardized my integrity, if Mom was going to stubbornly insist that I not only meet her suitors against my will but be nice about it, it seemed only reasonable she should do something to make the effort worth my while.

Chapter 54

At first, it was a mystery to me whether this fixation with Black men was entirely new for my mother or if there had always been latent interest she couldn't act upon for lack of diversity in New England. It seemed to be the latter.

According to Mom, it all traced back to one fateful day in 1969 when at the age of thirteen she'd seen her first interracial couple in Vermont. They were drifters whose route had brought them to the most unlikely of places: the quiet street my mother's family lived on. She and my grandmother watched intently out their living room window as the young Black man and his White companion slowly walked by, appearing road-weary from their travels. While neighbors retreated inside their houses to draw window shades closed, Grandma sprung out the door to invite the couple to dinner. Upon learning they were in the process of hitchhiking to Maine, she insisted that her husband drive them the rest of the way once they were refreshed by a hot meal. As my mother snuck peeks at their guests from across the dining table, she yearned to be the woman in that relationship and determined that one day she would.

It seemed to me that my parents' marriage was undermined from the very beginning by this pivotal experience. The way Mom characterized their love life, it was as though she and Dad had only been intimate five times, and each go at it had produced a child. This combination had silently but steadily eroded away the foundation of their relationship for eighteen years.

Chapter 55

In a bizarre twist, Dad sold the Issaquah house to his coworker Maude, who was in the process of divorcing her husband. He signed a lease at a one-bedroom apartment a half mile down the street from my mother's place. Ben and Heidi joined him, my brother sharing the bedroom with Dad using two twin beds, and my little sister sleeping on a pullout mattress in the loveseat, which was kept tucked behind an office divider at the far corner of the living room. Karina, Ryan, and I stayed put with Mom.

When the house went to Maude, her six-year-old daughter inherited my unfinished dollhouse, and they were also the involuntary new owners of the cat Mom had left behind. Some weeks later, Dad found out from Maude that because Kitty kept bringing dead mice into the house, upsetting her two young children, she'd given the cat away to some other family. When I learned the news, I sobbed into my pillow in the bed I shared with Karina.

"I miss her too," Mom said somberly.

You don't get to miss her! It's your fault she's gone! I wanted to scream. Instead, I just kept sobbing.

Chapter 56

Since Christmas had been a dud the previous year, on the heels of my parents' separation announcement, I wondered if we would get another crack at it this year. However, my parents didn't have the funds for gifts.

At this point, Mom was on food stamps. These kept our kitchen stocked with milk, breakfast cereal, and bread that we acquired from an Arnold's bakery outlet. The grocery store across the street didn't sell the major staples of our diet, and since Mom worked as a manager at a health food store, most of our groceries came from the marked-down section or the free bin in the employee break room. Our refrigerator contained wilted produce and soy products stamped with past sell-by dates.

If I knew Mom would be home all evening, I typically made a stir-fry for dinner. Given the random mix of foodstuffs on hand, they only made sense when cooked together in one pan with a generous douse of soy sauce. If I knew Mom would be going out after work, I just ate cereal and toast.

Renee encouraged me to get in touch with the local food bank. When I did, a courier arrived at our apartment with two paper bags filled to the top with nonperishable food items. While I was grateful for the service, I felt a distinctly teenaged sense of embarrassment as I extracted generic boxes and cans from the depths of the bags. Not a single item had a brand label on it: each package was stark white with black text, a clear indication to anyone who saw that it was government aid. No matter how unlikely it was that anyone would know what was in our cupboards, I felt ashamed nonetheless and didn't request the service again.

When Mom mentioned her financial predicament to Reginald, her personal trainer, he brought a colleague of his named Max into the conversation. The former, a bachelor, and the latter, a married father of two, were both financially secure. Together, they offered to buy each of Mom's children a gift so we could have some semblance of a holiday.

My mother came home from the gym in a great mood, cradling a three-foot-high artificial Christmas tree, excited to tell us the news. Placing the tree on the coffee table, she instructed me to start a list of the gifts we wanted, saying that Reggie and Max would take care of everything.

"Aren't they generous?" Mom said, smiling as she adjusted a few of the shiny red ornaments on the pre-decorated tree.

It was indeed exhilarating knowing I could have anything I wanted. Yet I felt like a sellout as I wrote down the one item I wanted more than anything: a pair of black Doc Marten boots with multicolored stitching that cost seventy-five dollars. I had seen them in a vintage clothing store in a Seattle neighborhood where all the punks and cool youth roamed. I could never have fathomed getting to own such an expensive pair of boots unless they were purchased for me by a couple of muscular men, one of whom was our very own personal homewrecker. It was anyone's guess as to whether the other man had slept with my mother—or just wanted to.

In Seattle, the '90s equivalent of '50s greasers all wore Doc Marten boots. I thought that if I also sported a pair, I'd attract friends and start getting to do all the great activities I was certain every teenager except me was doing.

On Christmas morning my siblings and I drifted sleepily out into the living room to find our gifts in all their glory stacked unwrapped around the base of the miniature tree on the coffee table. There were my Doc Marten boots, along with Ryan's video game console, Karina's brown suede bomber jacket, Ben's skateboard, and Heidi's doll.

While I cherished them, the boots did nothing to change my wallflower status. Every time I gazed upon them, I felt half pleased to have such a cool item in my wardrobe, and half guilty. I could have simply refused to put an item on the Christmas wish list, but what good would a smug moral superiority have done for me? Everyone else would have gotten exactly what they wanted, and no one would have been impressed with me for taking a stand.

I wondered how Dad would feel when he learned that other men had taken care of his children for Christmas. I imagined it would be emasculating. But then again, it might have come as a relief that he didn't have to do anything.

"Remember the year when you and Dad decided not to wrap our gifts?" I asked, recalling when I was eight. "You just put our gifts into piles, and we could all tell exactly which pile was meant for us?"

"Your father didn't do anything," Mom was quick to say. "Every holiday was planned and carried out by me."

I sat back in silence, digesting this unexpected insight. I'd always imagined my parents planning each holiday agenda together, excited about what they would do to bring magic into their children's lives. All this time I'd assumed that since Dad thought like a child, he was responsible for figuring out how to delight us, yet it had really been Mom behind the best surprises.

Chapter 57

I admired Karina for the trailblazing she had done as the eldest. Though she was only three years my senior, I couldn't recall ever having seen her behave like a child. I was never a lone wolf and preferred the safety of the pack, whereas my sister went out and found herself a job as soon as she was legally able, at fifteen-and-a-half, boldly entering the adult world of commuting, work shifts, and paychecks. I knew I couldn't do all that, as badly as I wished to earn money; I wasn't up to figuring out public transportation and navigating the confusing, chaotic adult world.

She had started at the movie theater and throughout the rest of high school maintained constant part-time employment. She bought her first car at sixteen with money she had earned herself. I longed to get a job to have spending money as well, so I found ways of earning cash like weeding a neighbor's yard, organizing Gloria's overstuffed closets, and continuing to babysit neighborhood children as I had been doing since seventh grade.

The collection of useless self-help books Mom had amassed soon after we moved to Washington was stacked on a shelf in her walk-in closet, left to collect dust. Each time I caught sight of them I sneered, for they hadn't prevented Mom from making what I felt were bad life decisions. When Karina and I were scheming ways to acquire extra spending money, we stole the entire collection and sold it to a used bookstore. We thought we had a big payload coming to us, but instead earned a measly seven dollars to split between the two of us for our efforts. Mom never noticed the book collection's disappearance, which confirmed my suspicions that they had been just a fad.

Once Mom was promoted to floor manager at Healthy Pantry, I got the opportunity to work at her store occasionally on weekends, stocking shelves. I got paid on the day of, in cash, an arrangement with which I was extremely pleased.

"Sweetie, if you can just unpack the boxes stacked at the end of this aisle, price the tops of the cans, and place them on the shelves here," she would politely instruct me. The track lighting above lit the golden highlights in her hair and the foundation on her skin with a radiating glow.

"Pete, you remember my daughter Angie," she would say, with her hand on my shoulder, whenever a colleague passed by. She would introduce me to her regular customers with the same pride, her blue-green eyes sparkling.

Inevitably, the other person would respond with: "Evelyn, you don't look old enough to have a teenage daughter!" I'd stand there and smile, as if it were my first time hearing such a statement.

"And can you believe my oldest is eighteen!" Mom would then say, beaming.

In the public sphere, her voice was an octave higher than at home, every exchange delivered with a smile. Public Mom was radiant, with a laugh as pleasant to the ear as wind chimes on a summer's day, a carefree laugh that told the world she did normal mom things like bake pie and take her children on picnics. Public Mom was precisely the mother I wished I actually had. I wondered why she only cared how people other than her children perceived her.

While Mom never lied to us, I felt she was lying to herself whenever she strove to perpetuate the image that she had her life in order. Anytime my siblings and I criticized her lifestyle, we were poking holes in the reality she was trying so desperately to construct.

Chapter 58

Although she wasn't around much, I had grown very attached to Karina and looked at her as a surrogate parent. When she decided to join the navy, it was deeply upsetting. I felt like I was being abandoned all over again. I threatened to go on a hunger strike unless Karina promised not to leave. But there was nothing to be done; she was contractually obligated to report to boot camp in Florida. I couldn't really go without the comfort of food, but for a whole week I managed not to let Karina or Mom witness me eat, thereby fooling them into believing I was truly starving myself.

The situation conjured up a memory of the one time I had succeeded in getting my sister to play make-believe with me when I was five years old. The pretense, chosen by eight-year-old Karina, was that we were an impoverished mother and daughter. Fighting for survival, we huddled together along the wall in our living room, where she wrapped a protective arm around me. We shivered against the imagined blasts of frigid air in a harsh landscape. "Don't worry, sweetheart," she said, in character. "I'll give you something to eat." She drew out an imaginary knife and pretended to carve away some flesh from her belly. "Here," she said, handing the invisible flesh to me, "eat this." At the time, all that crossed my mind was: *But we're vegetarian.* As a teenager, however, I found the level of parental concern she had demonstrated at such a young age extraordinary.

Now I was on a pretend hunger strike, grieving the impending loss of my sole ally.

"Please don't make this hard for me, Ang," Karina said. She pleaded with me to understand that she had to get away from our parents and was eager to earn the government's assistance paying for college. I was proud of her for finding a way out of the chaos at home but resentful about being left behind.

Since Karina had graduated high school and I was just a couple years away from it myself, I was suddenly aware for the first time that my parents hadn't planned to help their five children attend college. Yet they had moved us to what was known as one of the most highly educated regions in the country. That meant my siblings and I would all someday struggle to find employment the same as my parents had.

Despite the fact that my parents themselves were high school dropouts, I inferred that our education was important to them. This inference was largely due to their having moved to Heathburn from North Carolina so we could attend school at Satmardeva. Further, prior to my parents' separation, Dad used to bristle when any of us claimed to be ill and needed to stay home from school. "All right," he would say sternly, as though to let us know he was fully aware we were trying to pull the wool over his eyes, "but you're staying in bed all day and not getting to do anything fun." On family movie night in Vermont when we watched *Ferris Bueller's Day Off*, Dad left the room in disgust over the great lengths the protagonist went to in order to skip school.

⌇

Mom, having taught her children to eschew the entire medical establishment, was upset with Karina for permitting the military to inoculate her. She prided herself on having kept our bodies uncontaminated by giving birth to all of us at home with only my father present for assistance. Indeed, all five of us were incredibly healthy without having received any vaccinations, only catching the annual cold and flu as everyone did.

It annoyed me that while Mom had worked so hard, in her own way, to care for our bodies, she wasn't willing to extend the same level of concern for our mental well-being.

Meanwhile, Karina was berated by military officials who were scandalized by the fact that she'd never received even one vaccination in all her eighteen years of life. To catch her up, they injected her with a blast of everything in one go. She wasn't pleased about it but had no choice. Afterward, when she felt sick and developed a rash around the injection site, it gave Mom further ammunition to admonish my sister for her life choices.

Chapter 59

Aunt Gloria moved a few blocks southwest from where we'd lived in her basement. Occasionally I spent the weekend at her new house so that Jason and I could play Nintendo, watch movies, and eat junk food.

Having always had a soft spot for me, Gloria invited me to live with them. It was an enticing option, especially since she was in a better house in the best area of all of Bellevue, within walking distance to the lake and mall. However, as it was only a two-bedroom, it meant I would more than likely have to take a corner in her home office. And as much as I enjoyed her gregarious personality, I was sure my cousin was subjected to the same ear-searing details about his mother's social life as I was from my own.

Once when Gloria took Jason and me to Ocean Shores, a beach town on the Pacific Ocean, we three were sitting in a hot tub together. "You know what I like about being fat?" Gloria asked. I shook my head. "My boobs float to the top of the water, and they look great!" She chuckled with delight as she looked down. They were indeed buoyant.

I smiled politely and averted my gaze, while also avoiding eye contact with Jason, in case he felt embarrassed or uncomfortable.

I wasn't interested in trading life with my mother for a similar scenario under Gloria's roof. I didn't judge my aunt like I did my parents, though. At least she took care of her son. For good or bad, she was the same person out in the world as she was at home, while Mom only treated us nicely in front of company.

Deciding to stay put at Mom's apartment, I found myself for the first time in years with my own bedroom after Karina shipped out for boot camp. It was luxurious, although it took a few days to get used to having a bed to myself again.

Karina regularly kept in touch with me over the months she was gone. The first few letters, which relayed how she was getting on in boot camp, made it sound as though she were a POW: the early-morning drills, getting chewed out by her superiors if her bed sheets weren't tucked in tight enough to bounce a quarter off of, bathroom stalls with no doors, being forced to run long distances in shorts made of a scratchy, cheap material that chafed her thighs until she developed a rash, and the slop they served in the mess hall. Incidentally, Uncle Sam wasn't vegetarian-friendly, and she had little more to eat than peanut butter and jelly sandwiches and spaghetti.

A couple times when Karina was allowed to call home, she would tell me how badly she wished she could leave. I felt anxious for her, stuck there in such a challenging, unsupportive environment.

Immediately following the ten-week boot camp, she was transferred to a training facility in Virginia where her circumstances fortunately improved. She made friends, and the daily regimen was slightly more relaxed. She was in a facility where men outnumbered women twenty to one and, though she'd never been particularly feminine in demeanor or appearance, suddenly found herself with a barrage of suitors. The men, it seemed, were always looking for action. Though sex in the barracks was forbidden, Karina said everyone broke the rules. She overheard two women having sex in a bed not far from hers one night, and men and women found various ways of sneaking into each other's barracks. No one ratted anyone else out, she said.

Karina wrote me letters about how she and her friends frequented bars and got drunk whenever they were given leave of absence. Her reckless behavior made me fear for her safety, but it sounded like she was getting the college experience she'd wanted. I'd write back to remind her of our higher purpose as God's children. She would respond with more of the same stories.

Chapter 60

Like the cuckoo leaving its eggs in other birds' nests, Mom continually sought ways to shed her parental responsibilities. I overheard her on the phone with her youngest sister Linette, who lived in Kansas, trying to convince her to take Heidi and Ryan for the entire summer. I guess she hoped that her sister, having tried unsuccessfully for years to get pregnant with her husband, could be convinced to accept any child into her life.

After Dad moved to the Meadowbrook apartment complex down the street, the only occasion my parents spoke was when Mom called him to complain about how unfair it was whenever she had four children under her roof and he had just one. It was especially a sticking point if she had the two youngest with her.

Dad's response was always the same: "Turn them over to the state!"

Mom would hang up the phone growling and let loose a volley of insults designed to reflect poorly on Dad. "When I left your father, he asked me how I could abandon my children. He said he would never abandon them. And yet, where is he now?"

It tore me up inside to bear witness to these conversations and have it rubbed in my face that neither of my parents wanted us. It was painful to think how they made all their decisions clearheaded; their actions couldn't be blamed on drugs or alcohol. They simply just didn't want us anymore.

I was certain that Dad's intention had truly been to care for all five of us after Mom's departure. He probably thought he could raise us on his own. But when it proved harder than he thought, he withdrew.

"You know, your father wanted to have a vasectomy when he was in his twenties," Mom was fond of reminding us. "At the consultation, the doctor talked him out of it saying he might regret his decision someday. Now he's basically had one: no kids." She would finish the story, sounding jealous and embittered. It did not seem to stroke her ego that all five of her children preferred to stay with her; instead, it was clearly the bane of her existence that she just couldn't shake us.

I read how it was common for children to blame themselves for their parents' divorce. My conundrum was much larger: it was painful and confusing to contemplate what our role may have been in making our parents loathe not only each other but also their children. What had we done that was so terrible, so unforgivable that it caused their parental instincts to shut off? My best guess was that we had aggressively over-harvested without consideration of how the land would be replenished, and now it had dried up like a desert that would never see rain again.

On the first Mother's Day following my parents' separation, Mom seemed to indicate that her children might be at fault. Even after I had cooked her breakfast and stood ready to present her with a card I had spent hours making by hand, she said, "Why should anything matter today when it doesn't matter to you kids the rest of the year?" I was so hurt by her flippant comment that I decided then and there not to recognize the holiday again.

Regardless of the reason, shouldn't our parents continue to love us as their own flesh and blood, even if for no other virtue? How could Mom and Dad, who'd never missed a beat tending to our needs in Vermont, show so little interest in us now? Back then, I used to wonder how my parents could bear to behold my morning face, crusted over as it was with drool, creased from the pillowcase's seams, and beset with inexplicable puffiness below my eyes despite having gotten a sound night's sleep. Yet love me they did; no matter what, I could count on their love and care.

As part of their settlement, Dad was required to provide $300 a month to Mom for child support. However, he often failed to come through, and the court didn't enforce it. When I informed him of how we were struggling financially, he said he didn't want to relinquish any money to my mother since she'd just waste it on herself. I was disgusted with both his attitude and the fact that the state had dictated such a paltry amount to begin with. Aunt Gloria received $1,000 a month in child support for her single child. Of course, her ex-husband was a pilot and presumably had a much larger salary.

Every time I saw Dad now, he complained about how demanding my siblings were. He would provide an inventory of how much money each child had requested or the favors they asked of him, such as skateboarding sneakers for Ben and frequent rides to friends' houses for Heidi. If I mentioned needing money for anything, he reminded me that I was my mother's responsibility.

I thought about how the friends I'd had over the years who were children of divorce had gotten a far better deal. Where was my second bedroom in another house, my repeated holiday celebrations with two sets of gifts, and where was the evidence that my mother and father were vying to be perceived as the better parent?

When I complained to them about the state of things, they would respond with their own sad stories. Mom would say, "I told you that my mother used to slap my face until I was fourteen, right?" *Yes, you did*, I would think. Dad would say, "I told you my father said I wasn't wanted, right? He'd hoped my mother's fourth pregnancy would give him a daughter and not another son." *Yes, you did. Congratulations for perpetuating the abuse into the next generation*, I'd think.

Indeed, my parents had both suffered real childhood trauma. But I didn't want to hear about it in answer to my valid complaints about parental neglect in the present. Mom liked to say it's a wonder anyone survives their childhood and that no one does so without coming out of it mentally ill.

Like the parable of three blind men feeling different sections of an elephant and describing an entirely different experience, the grandparents I knew were very different from the parents Mom and Dad had known when they were growing up. In her golden years, my maternal grandmother couldn't pass a stranger without paying a compliment, and her husband had a ready chuckle to match the twinkle in his watery faded-blue eyes. He would present each of my siblings and me with a shiny silver dollar whenever they came up to Vermont to visit, and unknowingly lose more change in between the couch cushions for us to find later.

My paternal grandfather was a dapper man who kept his silver hair short and his face freshly shaven, pairing a suit with gleaming leather shoes every single day. When we visited him at his restaurant, Granddad would discreetly slip Andes chocolate mints to Ben and me, gesturing us over to the host's desk and glancing around dramatically before setting the candy into our upturned palms. We delighted in the feigned secrecy and wolfed down the chocolates with our backs turned even though Mom and Dad wouldn't have objected. Every year at Christmas, an enormous festive poinsettia was delivered to our door care of Granddad.

Did this mean that if I had children someday, my parents would be amazing grandparents to them? I would never know, as I'd already decided I didn't want to bring children into such a world.

Chapter 61

Given that my alternative high school didn't offer driver's ed, I wanted very badly to enroll in a private driving program that cost a whopping $350. Neither did I have the funds nor did I know what I would do with a license when I got it as I had no prospect of getting a car, no friends, and nowhere to go but away from my parents. Nevertheless, it was of the utmost importance to me as a fifteen-and-a-half-year-old that I attend this program simply because it represented freedom.

My father and his coworker Maude surprised me by offering to split the cost. I was stunned by their generous offer and the unusual arrangement but was also loathe to accept assistance from Maude. Dad had met her when he started as an assistant at the Montessori school. As the only man on staff, most of his coworkers were reserved around him. He had spoken of Maude at home, commenting on how she was the only welcoming one in the bunch.

On more than one occasion, Maude sent homemade peach cobbler home with Dad. Mom and Karina would raise an eyebrow at each other at its appearance on our kitchen counter. A slimy dessert, no one other than Dad partook, and most of it got dumped down the garbage disposal.

I didn't want to feel like I owed Maude anything. Thus, to earn their financial support, I arranged to help out three days a week at the preschool that they now ran together. While there, I refrained from initiating conversation with Maude about anything other than work-related topics, and she likewise didn't engage me in conversation about anything personal.

My first day on the job, I smiled at the sight of my father coming out of the kitchen carrying a latte in each hand in clear glass mugs. I was delighted that the tradition from the Issaquah house, when he had first purchased the espresso machine, had endured. I was about to reach out my hand to accept a mug, but when Dad's gait didn't slow, I turned to watch him pass the second latte to Maude, who was stooped down low helping a little boy with his paint set. She raised up to accept the mug, and I grimaced as she beamed at my father with more affection than was warranted from a coworker.

"Thank you, Bruce," she murmured with a cloying sweetness.

Maude tended to wear long-sleeved, ankle-length dresses in muted shades and old-fashioned prints. The hemline revealed color-coordinated tights stretched over sizable feet. Tall and willowy, she had large hands to match yet moved as silently as a deer trying to avoid detection in the brush. She reminded me of Nurse Ratched from *One Flew over the Cuckoo's Nest*, with her steady blue eyes, broad pale face, and long sandy-blond hair generally kept pinned up at the back of her head. In the film, empowered by the authority of her crisp white uniform, Nurse Ratched spoke calmly to gain the trust of the patients she tended in a mental asylum. By all outward appearances, she seemed an advocate for the powerless and suffering, when in actuality she maintained poise and chose her words deliberately to enforce order, nothing more. Because I didn't know what Maude's motives were, I didn't trust her. I felt an inexplicable jealousy and a desire to avoid her.

The driver's ed facility was a twenty-minute drive from Mom's apartment, requiring me to get rides to and from each class. Securing either parent's commitment was difficult, especially when I needed to be at any given place by a particular time.

One Saturday I'd walked to my father's apartment a half mile down the street and was waiting in his living room for him to return and give me a ride as promised. He was out somewhere with Maude, and since my younger siblings were at friends' houses, I stood alone in dreadful silence, staring out at the courtyard through the sliding glass doors that Dad would pass by when he arrived.

Heidi had let me in before leaving for her friend's house. I looked at the loveseat pullout mattress she slept on, positioned behind a plain Japanese screen in the living room. The apartment's single bedroom was shared by Dad and the boys. I didn't feel comfortable there, especially not by myself.

I was surprised when Dad still hadn't returned just before my class was scheduled to begin. The threat of arriving anywhere late caused me anxiety, often leading to a stomachache. Our instructor was adamant that students not miss any classes since it was a short-term, intensive program. I paced before the glass doors, pausing every few minutes to scan for movement outside.

I'm sure Dad will be here, I thought. *He won't let me down.* The scenario called to mind our family's first time celebrating Christmas at Granddad's place in Lake Charles, Louisiana, when I was about seven. Granddad lived in a two-story condo in the middle of a long, narrow brick building, surrounded by many others. From the outside, his condo looked just like the rest.

I was waiting for Ben to return. Moments earlier we had snuck out, down one of the winding concrete pathways that connected all the buildings. Huddling together, we'd lifted our palms to reveal the single sugar packet we'd each pocketed from the bowl next to the coffee maker. We grinned at each other before eagerly tearing our packets open. The paper crinkled loudly in the hush of the early winter morning as I poured its contents into my mouth. The granules stuck together at first in a clump, like sand. As they dissolved, I gulped the sweetness down.

"I'm gonna go get more!" Ben said.

I said I would wait outside, since our family would be leaving soon for breakfast at a nearby restaurant. In my brother's absence I stood and looked around at the rows of buildings angled like branches on a Christmas tree. The grass between the pathways wore a coat of glistening frost, but since the sky was pale blue, I knew it wouldn't snow. The sky always went gray before a snowstorm in Vermont.

I shivered inside my puffy gray coat. I hadn't expected it to be cold in Louisiana, even in December. My navy-blue corduroy pants and purple Puma sneakers weren't keeping me warm enough, and I wished my family would hurry up and join me outside. Shoving my hands deep into my pockets, I shrugged my shoulders up to my ears.

Nobody was coming to meet me on the pathway, so I started back toward what I thought was Granddad's place. I walked back and forth along the same row several times, unable to recall the house number.

My footsteps quickened as I frantically tried to find something I recognized. Heart pounding rapidly, I could see my breath as I sucked in the dry, crisp air through a wide mouth. I was afraid Mom and Dad would leave without me, not noticing I was missing. I stopped where I was and started to cry. If only I hadn't left the condo to eat sugar in secret, I would still be safe and warm with my parents and siblings.

Suddenly, I heard my father calling my name. He had come looking for me! I wasn't abandoned after all.

"Dad!" I shouted. "I'm over here!"

I spotted him down by the next building. He was wearing a beige wool fedora with a pinched front crown and a small pheasant feather sticking out of the hat band—a gift from his father—with his best winter coat. I ran to him and collapsed into his arms with relief when he knelt to comfort me.

When Dad finally returned to his apartment, it was too late for me to make it to class.

"I gotcha this," he said, with forced cheerfulness. He held out a small box of gourmet chocolates in his flat, upturned palm, the way you offer an apple to a horse so that it doesn't bite your hand. I accepted it from him with a frown.

"Thanks," I mumbled. "Dad, you know I was supposed to be at my driver's ed class twenty minutes ago?"

"Yeah, I'm sorry about that," he said. "But you'll catch up next week!"

"I'm gonna walk back to Mom's now," I said, collecting my notebook and pen. I resented my father's apology gift, preferring he had gotten me to class instead. But as I left his apartment, I knew I'd be tearing into the sweets as soon as I was in the privacy of my bedroom.

Chapter 62

Armed with a learner's permit, I pounced on any opportunity to practice driving. It was next to impossible to convince Mom to let me drive because she had her own things to do and wasn't about to waste her time letting me putter around aimlessly. On this occasion my mother had said, innocuously, that she needed to go to the store.

"Oh, please let me drive you!" I said. "I can only drive if the passenger is over twenty-one."

"All right," Mom conceded.

There had been a couple of occasions when Dad resigned himself to letting me practice in the used station wagon he bought after giving away the Volkswagen van that had broken down once and for all. His car was manual, however, and I couldn't get the hang of the clutch. At best I'd grind the gears, and at worst I'd stall out as I slowly drifted through his neighborhood's side streets. After each mistake I would grit my teeth and look over to the passenger seat to assess how badly I was doing. Dad usually had his eyes closed while resting his head against the seat, which meant no scolding but also no constructive feedback.

With Mom finally agreeing to chaperone, I slipped into the driver's seat, grinning. I buckled myself in and took a few minutes to adjust the seat, side mirrors, and rearview mirror as I'd learned in class. I successfully merged onto the highway, without hesitation, and shortly thereafter exited to pull into a parking lot according to Mom's instructions. As I carefully maneuvered the tiny two-door hatchback through the shopping plaza, I smiled upon recognizing the pet store where I'd gotten Teddy a year prior. The shopping complex also housed a grocery store, a coffee shop, an Indian restaurant, and a florist. I wondered which of these stores Mom had gone out of the way to shop at.

"Pull up here," she said, in front of Passion's Package. My heart sank. "I need to pick up a few things. You can wait in the car." She unbuckled her seat belt.

"I don't wanna wait here," I said, bristling at the thought of being the person who drove her mother to an adult store, then waited in the car directly outside the window like a weirdo. "I'll go with you," I said, thinking it the better alternative. She shrugged, and I followed her past the Eighteen and Older sign on the door.

As I trailed after my mother, I passed shelves containing lubes, self-pleasuring toys, edible thongs. "Wow," I whispered, "this place is disgusting."

"If you can't handle it, go wait in the car," Mom snapped. "I don't know why you came in anyway."

My mouth drew into a tight line. I pivoted on my heel and returned to the front of the store where it seemed safer. Hovering by the door, I avoided making eye contact with the cashier. *What in the world possessed me to think I could handle coming into such a place?* I asked myself.

As I watched the top of my mother's head bob amongst the racks of teddies, I had the sobering realization that my presence was likely an unwelcome reminder that her driver was waiting. I felt annoyed by the double standard: I couldn't have gone into the nearby pet store to kill time while Mom shopped, like I would have preferred, because if she finished first, she would be cross with me about having to wait. And I couldn't wait in the car as she had suggested, because she would feel she had all the time in the world.

I couldn't believe this was the same woman who had raised me from infancy, the one who used to have Victorian sensibilities and a utilitarian wardrobe. Which was my real mother—the wholesome wallflower I knew in Vermont or the self-absorbed woman who had replaced her? Had this alter ego always been present, incubating within Mom's subconscious until circumstances were right to emerge as the governing personality? It was a most unwelcome revelation that she had had a sex drive hidden behind those oversized glasses and Birkenstock sandals. This new mother was so image-conscious that if my siblings or I asked her for a ride somewhere once she was in for the night, she would say, "I can't. I've already taken out my contacts," preferring to be virtually blind over keeping a pair of glasses on hand for emergencies.

On the next occasion I convinced Mom to let me drive, she was headed downtown to Dez's apartment. This time Mom ordered me to stay put as soon as I'd parked.

"I'll only be a few minutes," she said.

It dawned on me that I had escorted my mother to a sexual rendezvous.

"I shouldn't have driven here!" I exclaimed, gripping the steering wheel in frustration. "What am I gonna do?"

"I don't know," Mom said, one foot already out the door. "Drive back home if you want."

As much as I longed to leave, the fear of getting caught driving without a driver's license was enough to keep me there. If I were to get pulled over, it might mean losing the privilege of getting a driver's license in the first place, or worse, it could go on my permanent record.

"I'll just wait here," I grumbled, watching as Mom shut the passenger door and disappeared up a staircase. I rolled my window down and sighed.

Reappearing twenty minutes later, Mom waved coyly to Dez, who was presumably watching her leave. He wasn't in my line of sight, which meant I also wasn't in his. I wondered whether Mom had told him I was waiting in the car. I doubted that came up in their pillow talk.

Mom climbed into the passenger seat with a satisfied smile on her face.

"Dez keeps a pet python in a massive cage in his living room," she announced. "It'd love to eat Teddy!"

I gritted my teeth while gripping the steering wheel. I decided I wouldn't ask Mom to let me drive her places anymore.

After parking at our apartment complex and exiting the car, Mom caught the eye of a young Black man riding up the sidewalk on his bicycle. He couldn't have been much older than me. He ogled my mother, as every man seemed to do now that she oozed sexuality. Mom threw an arm high in the air and enthusiastically waggled her fingers at him.

"Woohoo!" she squealed, shimmying her shoulders. I grimaced and looked away.

Later that week, I returned home from school to find I didn't have my key on me. When knocking didn't bring anyone to the door, I noticed Dez's Porsche out front. I sat down on the top step and glumly dropped my chin into my hands.

It occurred to me that if I hadn't forgotten my key, I would have overlooked the Porsche's presence in the parking lot and could have had an awkward encounter inside the apartment.

"Hello there," Dez said in his booming voice. I looked up to see him smiling down at me.

"Hi, sweetie," Mom said, holding onto the frame of the door as she leaned out. "I didn't know you were out here."

I rose and pressed my back against the banister to allow Dez plenty of room to maneuver his bulky frame down the stairs. As a power lifter, his arms didn't lay flat along his sides; they hovered at a distance on account of his barrel chest and oversized biceps. Mom waved after him as I ducked inside the apartment.

Chapter 63

After only a few months at the Meadowbrook apartment complex, Dad shocked us all by buying a house with Maude. He had yet to officially announce that he and Maude were a couple. They were suddenly becoming homeowners together, and it was up to us to infer what we might from the arrangement.

Mom and I learned the news from Ben, who was the only child continuously living with Dad. Both Heidi and Ryan alternated between our parents' homes. I felt blindsided yet again by developments I hadn't seen coming.

"I knew it!" Mom said. "Your father was probably having sex with her before I even left him."

As soon as Dad was settled and Mom could foist children onto him for a weekend, she delivered Heidi, Ryan, and me to his doorstep.

Pulling into the driveway, I saw that their house was positioned above a sloping yard. A playground had been constructed, not for Dad's own children but for strangers. The grass had been stripped away and replaced with gravel. The swing set and jungle gym were secured in an impractical cascading manner down the hillside with their posts set in concrete and surrounded by a plastic playhouse and other equipment. I shuddered at the view, picturing all the skinned knees bound to occur there amongst all that steel, concrete, and gravel.

Touring the inside, I found that the interior was also optimized to be enjoyed by other people's children, those who attended Dad and Maude's in-home preschool. While to me the place felt cold, both in spirit and temperature, for the students it was a veritable funhouse. The common areas were devoid of personal effects or normal-sized furniture. Instead, the Montessori-inspired layout was complete with child-sized tables and chairs, sensory experience stations, and easels. To my dismay, our family's collection of colorful National Geographic books lined the shelves.

The house had three bedrooms: the primary bedroom, shared by Dad and Maude; the one farthest from the primary, occupied by Ben; and the one in between, used for storing school supplies.

I looked around for our heirloom dining table and yellow couch but didn't see either. When I inquired about them, Dad said that he'd left them by the dumpster when he moved out of his apartment. He said another family was watching from their patio and rushed to retrieve the items as he walked away.

My father had razed a forest to make way for saplings. For him, I'm sure it was a practical matter—the old furniture didn't belong in this world of miniatures. But it felt spiteful.

How could you? You had no right! I wanted to scream. Instead, I asked eagerly, "Why didn't you offer it to us?"

"I did," Dad said. "Your mother didn't want it."

I reeled in the revelation that unlike me, my parents had zero sentimental attachment to any vestige of our life in Vermont. I alone mourned the loss of our family unit, traditions, and possessions. The last connection we had to the tight-knit family we used to be, the sacred place where we had gathered time after time to enjoy meals together, had been left in a trash heap. At the very least, I thought that Dad would have saved the table if only for the photo of our guru prominently displayed on it.

Between the two of them, Dad and Maude had ten offspring. According to a passing comment made by my father, Maude's three oldest refused to speak to her after she left their father. The two youngest had lived with her at our old Issaquah house that she'd purchased after we moved out. Once she and Dad moved in together, they returned to their father. Just as my siblings and I had rejected Maude, her children apparently refused to acknowledge my father.

There was something very wrong with this picture: two people with ten children combined weren't on good terms with any of them, and none of their kids wished to live with them. While Ben resided with Dad and Maude, he certainly didn't enjoy it or feel like part of a family. I fantasized about revealing to the parents of Dad's students that they were entrusting their offspring to people who didn't care about their own children.

If the word "stepmother" was even once uttered in that house, it had immediately been snipped out of the air like a dialogue bubble from a comic strip, crumpled up, and thrown into the garbage can, just as likely by Maude as by any of my siblings. There was no *Brady Bunch* scenario in our future.

It sent shivers down my spine to hear Maude giving instructions to my younger siblings; each carefully phrased statement struck my ear as manipulative. She was never going to fool me with that soft tone, which I figured was why she didn't bother addressing me beyond obligatory greetings.

After the emotional blows my father had received from his ex-wife and children, it seemed he sought respite with someone who kept not only her own tongue and emotions in check but also those of the people around her. She created a nearly impenetrable force field around my father, which I imagined made him feel safe from the emotional tide lapping dangerously close from the other side.

Dad and Maude neither invited us to join them for meals nor offered to cook for us. Once they had eaten their dinner and retired for the evening, Ben showed us how he made calzones for himself using instant pastry mix. After heaping shredded cheese and marinara sauce in the middle of a flattened disc of dough, which was then folded over to form a crescent, he popped it into the oven.

The kitchen was primarily stocked with economy-sized containers of juice, animal crackers, and paper cups. Ben told me that the good stuff was rationed: Dad issued him one can of soda per day from a plastic storage container that also held chips and cookies, kept sealed with a lock in his bedroom. Once when Dad and Maude were out of the house, Ben managed to pry up one corner of the chest's lid just enough to force one hand through and sneak an extra soda.

Chapter 64

One afternoon Mom was chatting on the phone with Gloria while seated next to me on the couch. I laid my head on her leg, and she stroked my hair as the two sisters conversed about their parents whom they and their other siblings referred to as "Mother and Dad." I'd always found it interesting that the titles implied a closer relationship with one parent over the other. I remained motionless in a half-conscious state, enjoying the physical contact. Once the phone call concluded, I sat up.

In unusually good spirits, Mom leaned forward and lovingly cupped my chin in her hand. "You're so beautiful," she said, beaming at me. I melted into her hand, smiling bashfully and wondering what I had done to earn such praise.

"God, you look just like me!" Mom exclaimed, sitting back against the couch cushion, her blue-green eyes sparkling. "It must drive your father crazy to feel like he's still staring right at me every time he looks at you!" She let out a shrill, spiteful laugh.

I pulled away, frowning. I didn't appreciate the false compliment. Everyone knew I looked more like Dad anyway, with his hair and eye coloring and high forehead.

⁓

Every now and again Mom would rant about how she never got any time to herself and couldn't handle having kids around. She would force me and any other children under her roof to spend the weekend at Dad's house, which I was loathe to do because I didn't want to acknowledge Maude in our lives. It felt awkward asking my father if I could stay with him when we weren't even on good terms.

On one such weekend when I was at Dad's place, Ben and I were going to watch *The Rocky Horror Picture Show* on the small television set with a built-in VCR in his bedroom. When Dad seemed receptive, we would make overtures to him. On this occasion, we invited him to watch the movie with us.

Ben and I were sitting on the lower half of his bunk bed as the video started, and when Dad came in with Maude on his heels, they proceeded to sit on the floor with their backs against the side of the bed. Ben and I grimaced at each other with dismay about the uninvited guest.

As soon as Dr. Frank N. Furter came on screen in his fabulous corset and heels, Maude whispered something to my father and left the room. Dad instantly sprung to his feet.

"Where are you going?" I asked.

"Uh, Maude doesn't want to watch the movie," he said meekly and hurried after her.

I felt disgusted by his behavior, especially since we'd issued the invitation only to him. He would do as Maude wanted, and it seemed evident she was intentionally driving a wedge between him and his children. If she had ever even once extended an effort to make us feel welcome in their house, Dad probably would have followed suit.

Another time, when Ryan and I were both there sleeping over in Ben's room, we were all still wide awake at midnight. Full of energy, we decided that since it was a mild temperature outside and the sky was lit by a full moon, we'd go play on the massive playground on the front lawn. As Ryan was goofing around, he slipped on the gravel, rolled downhill, and banged into a metal pole. Blood gushed from his nose, and he began wailing.

"Shh!" I coaxed. "Keep it down! We're going to get in trouble. C'mon, let's go to the bathroom."

We all three rushed into the main bathroom, unfortunately located directly outside my father's bedroom. Ryan continued to whimper as I sat him down on top of the toilet lid and pressed a wad of tissues against his nose.

Ben and I stared at each other upon hearing my father's bedroom door swing open.

"What the hell is going on?" Dad said, looming over us as we cowered around the toilet.

"Ryan fell and hurt his nose," I stammered.

"Well, keep it down!" he snapped. "I've got work in the morning."

Chapter 65

"So what's it like over at your father's?" Mom would ask when I returned from visits to Dad's house.

"Cold. And everything is set up for the preschool kids," I said, not wanting to have this conversation with her. "We didn't spend much time there; Ben and I walked down to the grocery store—"

"And where was Maude?" Mom cut in.

"Oh, I don't know. I guess she just stayed in the bedroom. Anyway, Ben and I—"

"How do they act together? I bet they both look so old! Can you believe I used to be married to your father? We don't look like we'd go together at all, right?"

"Um-hm," I said. "Anyway, there's this park nearby that we like to go to—"

"What's their bedroom like?"

"I haven't seen it."

"What about Maude's kids? Do they ever come over?"

"Not that I know of."

"And what about her ex-husband? Do you know anything about him?"

"No."

"I always felt that your father was already up to something with Maude well before I left. I'm just glad I left when I did."

I could tell from the eager look on Mom's face that she wanted me to spill the dirt. But not only was there no dirt—I was also uncomfortable with the line of questioning. I felt as though she were trying to plant a spy in Dad's house each time she forced me over there.

It bothered me how Mom liked to pretend that Dad had designs on his coworker before Mom cheated on him, as though to alleviate her own guilt. There was clearly a lot I didn't understand about the world, but one thing I knew for certain was that Dad would've been faithful to her until the end if they'd stayed married. It wasn't sporting of her to insult the person who got left in the marriage.

Chapter 66

Mom determined that we needed to confront my father about his failings as a parent. Insisting that my siblings and I participate, she drove us over to his house to ambush him. All the way there, my stomach was in knots.

Since Dad and Maude were out, we took a seat at the shaded patio table behind their house and waited. As soon as they pulled up the driveway, they saw us. Maude headed straight into the house without a word. After Mom announced we were there for a family meeting, Dad dropped resignedly into a chair opposite us without removing his sunglasses or cap.

Mom started in on him for not being a present parent. Then she encouraged each of us kids to share whatever was on our minds. I called my father out for not making an effort to connect with his children anymore, as evidenced by the fact that he wouldn't even remove his sunglasses to look us in the eye. He whipped them off his face and tossed them onto the table, giving me a hard look. My stomach continued churning, and I wanted to turn and run for the safety of our car. Somehow my mother wielded the power to rally us all to her cause, even when it was the last thing we wanted to do.

Chapter 67

I longed for a sweet sixteen birthday, the kind of party I was certain all those girls I used to be friends with at Newport High would have been given by their parents, complete with decorations, friends, and an over-the-top celebratory ambiance that would make the birthday girl feel fortunate and popular. What I got fell far short of the fantasy: the only people to attend were Dad and my sisters, Karina having returned from basic training. Mom was working that day, and Ben and Ryan were out with friends. Since I'd fallen out of touch with everyone I knew at my previous schools, there wasn't anyone else to invite.

An uneasiness hung in the air as soon as Dad arrived at the apartment. I was surprised he was even willing to enter Mom's space. It was likely a commitment he gave Karina, who had been the one to invite him, only after assurances that Mom wouldn't be present. He looked around nervously after sitting down at the table in the living room. Then he handed me an unwrapped bright-teal pullover sweatshirt. As I took it into my hands and pretended to admire it, I was dismayed that he wasn't aware I was very particular about color. I supposed he hadn't noticed I preferred darker shades, like burgundy, and never wore anything that loud. He had likely picked it up wherever he bought his own generic clothes.

Karina gave me a white coffee mug with an image of rainforest plants painted on the side. She showed me how, once filled with hot liquid, the sweeping green leaves in the forefront magically disappeared to reveal an orange-toed tree frog. Obsessed with rainforests and the idea of traveling to Costa Rica, I found the mug charming. However, neither of my two gifts nor the act of sitting awkwardly in relative silence around the dining table with just three family members present lived up to my expectations for my sixteenth birthday, and I felt shorted an important rite of passage.

My older sister hadn't received a sweet sixteen birthday either. I had chalked it up to the fact that we were living in Gloria's basement at the time. Although a positive precedent hadn't been set in our family, I had maintained hope of being pleasantly surprised.

Chapter 68

One morning I realized with horror that I'd left my diary on the living room coffee table overnight. Upon noticing it out in the open, I clutched it to my chest, feeling violated. En route to returning the notebook to its rightful place in my bedside table drawer, I passed Mom in the hallway.

"I forgot my diary in the living room," I said. "Did you look in it?"

"No," she said sharply, as though the accusation was preposterous. She continued going about her business getting ready for work.

As I restored the notebook to the depths of the drawer, I felt relieved that no one had seen my innermost thoughts. Yet I simultaneously felt annoyed. *Why doesn't Mom care enough to sneak a peek?* I thought.

Chapter 69

An abused dog doesn't wonder why he is mistreated by his owner; he just wants the behavior to stop. That's how it was for me at first. But with time, I not only questioned the cruel treatment we received at our parents' hands but also manifested the stress in myriad ways.

I had been suffering a recurring nightmare that I was in a van with my family, as the driver. My view was obstructed because the driver's seat was situated in the middle of the van. With my siblings sitting in the rows of seats in front of me, I had to crane my neck to see around their heads, desperately attempting to safely steer us to our destination. The anxiety was so palpable, I could still feel the tension throughout my body when I awoke.

~

Heidi was the only other person at home when I decided to walk to the park to smoke. Even after observing my frown and irritable demeanor, she insisted on accompanying me. She struggled to keep up with my furious gait.

"What if Mom gets AIDS?" I said, having learned she didn't use contraceptives. AIDS was a scare tactic created by the government, she'd told us; how could she contract something she didn't believe in?

"I think about that too," Heidi said.

I reached into the pocket of my army jacket and wrapped my fingers around the pack of Marlboros I'd purchased at the gas station across the street without the clerk asking for identification. I ran my forefinger and thumb back and forth across the smooth plastic wrap. My smoking habits were irregular; I only indulged when I felt at my worst.

Once we reached the park, Heidi climbed to the top of the jungle gym. I stood at a respectful distance and kept my back to her as I pulled a cigarette from my pocket. I felt my sister's huge brown eyes trained on me. When I looked back, I saw that she was weeping silently as her light brown hair hung limply around her pale, narrow face.

Lighting the cigarette, I stared off into the distance and shifted my weight from foot to foot as my mind churned over the mess my parents had made of our family.

I'd learned from Mom that she had never actually been able to convince Dad that moving away from Vermont was a good idea. This knowledge cast an even darker shadow over the string of failures that had beset our family since the cross-country move. It had come down to her telling him she was going with or without him. Dad followed his wife, naturally, and my siblings and I had no choice but to go wherever our parents went, trusting that they had our best interests at heart.

Everything about the move was predicated on a false premise: that Mom and Dad were on the same page, had a solid relationship, and had the finances to sustain us through a relocation. There was precedence for believing that Mom thought ahead, with the earliest evidence being that whenever our family was on the verge of leaving for vacation or driving south to visit relatives, she opened all the windows to let in fresh air and insisted that each of us pitch in to conduct a deep clean so that we'd return to an orderly house. Yet when it had really counted, it appeared that no planning or preparation whatsoever had been conducted beyond my parents trading in the house and business for seven one-way tickets to Washington. It was now clear that our family was never set up for success in the first place. No wonder things had turned out the way they did.

Given the consequences of the cross-country move, it pained me to think how I had given Mom my consent to move. By appealing to my siblings and me at our level, she had awakened an unfounded curiosity for what lay on the other side of the country when all our needs were already met in Vermont. It felt like bait and switch; she had dangled the possibility of a Disneyland trip before our wide-eyed faces simply to win our agreement to move to the West Coast, after which she didn't so much as feign interest in delivering on her promise. I had failed to protect myself by allowing Mom to convince me there was something better out there in the world.

Stuck between a rock and a hard place, Dad must have had a terribly unsettling decision to make: whether to watch his wife leave him or follow her into the unknown, where she ended up leaving him anyway. I finally understood why he was so bitter. He had sacrificed everything and gotten nothing in return. I would be inconsolable too if I were in his shoes. Of course, Mom had also struggled, contending with the hard work of raising children ever since she herself was a teenager, running a home business, and not getting the emotional support she needed from Dad. But none of these circumstances excused their actions, and the revelation that my parents had so haphazardly mortgaged their children's futures left me outraged.

I lit a second cigarette and tossed the spent one into a nearby garbage can. Pacing back and forth, I contemplated whether my family's karma made us fall apart. If I were to stumble and break my arm, I would be certain that my karma made it happen. But where free will was concerned, I didn't see how that interacted with karma at all. My parents chose to move and how to conduct themselves following the move. It wasn't thrust upon them by something outside of their control like foreclosure or illness. It was free will that had landed us in this tangle. Perhaps the only true free will was how one responds to stimuli. Still, in our case, Mom initiated the cross-country move, and Dad acquiesced (however begrudgingly). So it seemed to all come down to poor decisions with some bad luck thrown in. It was all avoidable, had we remained in Vermont.

I thought about the time I discovered a nest in our shed when I was about four years old. Curious to get a glimpse of the baby birds I heard chirping above my head, I used a stepladder to get closer. It didn't put me up quite high enough, so I gently tipped the nest toward me. Either I pulled too hard, or it wasn't well secured. It plummeted to the ground. I climbed off the ladder and looked down at the three chicks that had stopped chirping. Their tiny bodies with short gray feathers and bald heads lay unmoving upon the earth. I felt no sadness or remorse because I didn't understand what I had done.

Mom's inclination to follow her every whim was akin to me wanting to see inside that nest at any cost. Only she didn't have the excuse of childhood innocence; she should have known better. And in her oversexed state, she had stolen what was rightfully mine: the leeway afforded teenagers to try new things, make mistakes, and know there is always safety and support to be found at home.

I thought about how, at the very least, I had benefited from a solid childhood foundation in Vermont, but Heidi and Ryan were so young when we left that they never really knew the good years. All they would remember was the post-separation nightmare, and I worried about their well-being. On several occasions I considered calling Child Protective Services, but the mere thought of my siblings and me assigned to different foster homes gave me chills. I didn't want to incur their resentment for bringing that upon us. More than that, fear of the unknown—turning our fate over to strangers, losing touch with each other, and the abuse that children sometimes suffer in foster care—far outweighed the neglect I knew at home.

As I took the final drag off my cigarette, I wished Heidi and I had stayed at the apartment and played a board game instead of me complaining aloud about the injustices wrought upon us by our parents and smoking in front of her. I realized I was guilty of doing the same thing to her that our mother did to us—exposing her to that which was beyond her understanding or responsibility to bear.

Chapter 70

Things turned around for me when I learned from my childhood friend Alyssa that her grandmother had offered to buy me a plane ticket to enable the two of us girls to spend the summer together. I requested the soonest flight possible in order to enjoy ample time throughout the remainder of July and the entire month of August.

As I prepared for my trip, Karina agreed to care for Teddy, and Ben was in the process of moving into Mom's living room. By that point fifteen, he had been wiling away his afternoons with his skateboarding crew at a local Denny's, where they would each purchase a single cup of coffee and sit for hours smoking and drinking bottomless refills. Afterward, they would skate in the parking lot. When the restaurant manager caught on, they were banned from the property. Ben had also taken to storing liquor on his closet shelf, leaving the door wide open in hopes that Dad would discover it and show concern.

Outside of the common areas, my father and Maude either remained confined to their bedroom or went out together, never extending an invitation to Ben. On weekend mornings, my brother would awaken to find a note taped to the fridge that said, "Flew the coop."

After this living arrangement went on long enough, Ben told Dad that they needed to have a talk, as he was tired of being ignored. Though he received Dad's agreement to a sit-down after preschool let out for the day,

Ben glanced out his window in time to witness Dad coasting down the driveway in his car before starting up at the bottom of the hill.

According to Ben, this was a common practice so that Dad wouldn't tip my brother off to his escape. Ben was so angry that he punched a hole in his bedroom wall. When Dad discovered the damage, he ordered my brother out of the house. So Ben and Karina switched places.

Chapter 71

In July 1993, I returned to Vermont by way of Logan Airport in Boston. Alyssa's parents collected me on their way up to their summer house. As they would have to return to Natick a few times throughout the summer, my plan was to divide my time between their place in Heathburn and my uncle Eldon's house.

One night I dreamt I encountered my three-year-old self. She looked just as I had in photos of that age: a small frame, a chubby round face, and wispy golden-brown hair that splayed into loose curls at the ends. I knelt down, smiling at her. She approached me shyly at first, as a child does when meeting someone new. Then she walked into my open arms, which I wrapped around her tenderly. I felt such compassion for her that when I awoke, I had a sense that I had experienced healing on a subconscious level.

As I sat on the back porch of Alyssa's summer house the next day, staring out at the dense green foliage, I realized I felt only dread at the thought of returning to Washington. Following my family's relocation to the West Coast, I had never felt like I belonged anywhere. The caring parents who would thoughtfully lay a blanket over me after I fell asleep on the couch no longer had any concern for my well-being.

It occurred to me that I was old enough now that I didn't have to keep letting my fate remain in the hands of others, especially those who didn't have my best interests at heart. It was time I started guiding my life in the direction I felt appropriate. I wished for nothing more than to graduate from my old school, craving the discipline and structure that Satmardeva offered. I was ready to return to the fold, even if it meant going it alone.

I thought back to Dad's prescient words that I would change my mind someday about wanting to live with him forever. I hadn't believed him at the time—hadn't *wanted* to believe him. I certainly never would have expected it to occur this soon, but there I was, leaving home at sixteen.

Despite it being August, I managed to get in contact with the school's admissions counselor, Judy, and arranged to apply. She was a member of my spiritual community who had lived close by, so I knew her well. With long salt-and-pepper hair, Judy had a radiant smile and cheerful energy that she had employed to support students at the school ever since it was founded. Eager to help in any way she could, she fast-tracked the review of my application, no small favor considering that the process was typically conducted in the spring. She told me I was fortunate to be applying for entry to the junior class; if I were just one grade lower or higher, they wouldn't be able to entertain my application due to already being at maximum capacity with fifteen students in each.

Chapter 72

During the first of the periods when Alyssa and her parents needed to return to Massachusetts, I decided to surprise Eldon at his house. I hadn't informed him about being in Vermont. After getting dropped off at the end of his driveway by Alyssa's mother, I surveyed Eldon's extensive property. It was apparent my uncle had finally completed work on the house, which he had built from the foundation up. There was a small garden out front, and the row of baby pine trees planted along the road were in the process of growing to form a privacy hedge for their yard. The garage had a two-door Honda hatchback and a small pickup truck parked in it.

When Eldon answered my knock at the door, he beamed. "Angie!" he said, without so much as a pause to identify the unexpected visitor on his doorstep. I smiled into his shoulder as he gave me a warm embrace. It was the closest I'd felt to normal in years.

Aside from his hair having gone fully gray, Eldon looked just as I remembered, with the same lean frame and neatly trimmed beard. Magnified by his glasses, his soulful brown eyes looked disproportionately large in his long, narrow face. He had the softest voice of anyone I'd ever known.

My cousin Alan stood off to the side, gawking at me. He didn't smile or initiate a hug. Though he was only a year younger than me, we'd never gotten along well. He didn't get on with anyone as far as I'd ever been aware. It was weird to see he had become a man. When he finally spoke to greet me, it was in a deep voice I'd never heard from him before. He had curly brown hair, beady brown eyes, and an unsmiling round face. His gangly limbs still had the same inhuman way of moving when he walked, rather like C-3PO, the droid from the *Star Wars* films.

"Hi, Alan," I said.

"Hi," he replied.

Their family lived in a two-story house. As we caught up, Eldon explained that he and his wife maintained bedrooms on separate floors. Arlene restricted her movements to the main floor, and Eldon only entered that area to do laundry and access the kitchen.

Chapter 73

Less than a week before I was scheduled to return to Washington, I received word of my admittance to Satmardeva School and a full scholarship. I had just days to consider my answer and determine the logistics of how exactly I could stay on in Vermont. Remaining there meant being apart from my siblings with no assurance of getting to see them for the next two years, but returning to Washington meant suffering neglect and little hope for a good future.

The condition to my scholarship was that I would be responsible for cleaning the main floor of the high school building each weekend. It included a library, three classrooms, and one bathroom. I appreciated that they gave me an opportunity to help pay my own way, however small, so that I wouldn't feel like a freeloader.

Growing up I'd thought that having four siblings meant I would always be surrounded by family. Even if our parents couldn't be counted on, we would always have each other. But we had begun drifting apart immediately after my mother and father separated, as we each processed the traumatic experience differently. It had been the most painful experience of my life to watch the dismantling of my family play out. My impending self-exile in Vermont would be the most extreme realization of this new world order, exceeding even Karina's absence for military training, though through her trailblazing she had in effect paved the way for me to make this decision for myself. It was clear to me that this was my shining opportunity to get off the sinking ship, as my tenth-grade counselor Renee had repeatedly encouraged me to do.

I knew Eldon would be passing by Alyssa's house on his way home from work that afternoon, and I loitered at the end of the driveway until I saw his truck coming down the dirt road. He pulled up alongside the edge of the driveway, smiling, and I bounded over to his open window.

"Guess what! I got into Satmardeva!" I said, clasping my hands under my chin.

"Congratulations!" Eldon said, smiling. Like rays of sun breaking out from behind a cloud, the creases at the outer edges of his soulful brown eyes instantly multiplied.

"I want to accept and stay in Vermont," I said, waiting to see what he would say next.

"You can stay with me."

"I can? Are you sure?" I gushed.

"Yes," he said. "I don't know what Arlene will have to say about it, but either way, you're welcome to stay with me upstairs."

"Oh, thank you so much, Eldon!" I said. "I'm so excited! I can't believe it."

He chuckled, his right arm resting casually across the top of the steering wheel and the left along the window frame.

"I'm going to call Judy back now," I said, "and tell her that I accept their offer."

"Okay," Eldon said. "Congratulations again. That's wonderful news. I'll talk to you later."

As he drove on, I raced back inside Alyssa's house to the phone to share the news with my mother. I felt proud for advocating for myself.

"Guess what!" I said when Mom answered. "I've decided to stay in Vermont, and I've been accepted to Satmardeva!"

"Don't you think you should be asking my permission?" she said.

I paused, astounded. I didn't know what I'd expected, certainly nothing as standard as a congratulatory response. The first response that came to my mind was, *No, you gave up the right to be treated like a parent when you stopped acting like one*, but I didn't have the guts to say it out loud. I had half expected her to be happy to at long last have succeeded in getting rid of at least one child, but perhaps she was annoyed at losing the one who served as babysitter and maid.

"No," I said, frowning. "I'm responsible for myself." I had so badly wanted to keep the conversation light.

"Oh," Mom said, as if it were news to her.

"Anyway," I continued, "I arranged to clean the school on weekends to cover the tuition."

"That's good. Do what you have to," she said. "Well, I went to see a psychic this past weekend because I'm trying to decide whether to have a baby with Winston or Darnell."

Heidi had already informed me of the latest boyfriend, whom Mom met at an adult store where Darnell was a salesclerk. My sister described him as socially awkward and tall, with a completely shaved head except for a round puffball at the back. When we talked about it over the phone, we giggled and speculated at what was behind his odd hairstyle choice: was he a Hare Krishna? A hippie? Or just bad at cutting his own hair?

Since Mom's social interactions occurred only at the gym, all her suitors had similar characteristics: chiseled, image-conscious men who exuded confidence. Once she began meeting men at dance clubs, bars, and at work, the type began to vary. The one constant was that they were always Black.

"I always wanted to have a Black baby," Mom continued.

I rolled my eyes. Considering she didn't want any of the children she already had, how dare she insult us with the absurd consideration of a sixth child? How detached was she from reality that she'd want to subject another innocent life to this madness my siblings and I had to suffer at her hands? And why on earth would she want to have a baby with any of the men in her long string of obviously short-lived, unstable relationships? There wasn't much she could say that shocked me anymore, but she had succeeded with this bombshell of a revelation.

As Mom rambled on about the specifics of her conversation with the psychic, I stopped listening. Before picking up the phone to make the call, I had determined not to allow my good news to be derailed under any circumstances. As anger gave way to disappointment, tears streamed down my face, even as I chastised myself for getting emotional. Had I really thought I could escape the crazy simply by moving away?

Chapter 74

Since one end of Eldon's house was built into a hill, exiting from the second floor still meant being at ground level. I never witnessed my aunt and uncle so much as crossing paths outside. I figured they were familiar enough with each other's schedules that they could time their comings and goings so they wouldn't have to see each other.

When I gleefully informed Arlene that Eldon had invited me to stay, she told me in hushed tones of her concerns that since things weren't right between her and Eldon, it wasn't a good idea for me to be there.

My aunt was a brunette who still maintained an old-fashioned bouffant hairdo by sleeping on curlers at night, which seemed an odd length to go to for someone who didn't even wear makeup. Pale skinned, she never failed to don a floppy straw hat when going out to the garden to pick vegetables. Although slim and of average height, all her clothing was loose fitting, as though she hadn't updated her wardrobe since the seventies. She favored dark polyester slacks that hung wide at the ankle paired with sleeveless silken A-line tops extending modestly past her waistline. Upon standing, she always gave two quick tugs to her blouse's hem at either hip to ensure not a stitch was out of place. With the motion of a windup toy, she habitually used the knuckle of her right forefinger to chuck her large rimless glasses up the bridge of her sharp nose.

I relayed my conversation with Arlene to Eldon, asking whether I should find another place to live.

"I can't believe she told you that," he said. "This is my house!"

The next day, Eldon pulled a huge sheet of plywood over the top of the stairs to further delineate his territory.

"There," he said, "now you're staying with me and not her."

I felt bad about worsening the rift between them, but their relationship had never been good for as long as I'd known them. Though Eldon had moments where the sun peeked out from behind the clouds, he was solemn and silent most of the time, appearing resigned to the notion that everything in life was stacked against him. The sunken skin below his cheekbones made him appear much older than fifty.

Just like the stair-covering, the walls, ceiling, and floor were bare plywood; it was more of an unfinished attic made livable with two carpeted bedrooms, a full bathroom, and a makeshift kitchen like we'd had in Gloria's basement. Working with a refrigerator, a two-burner hot plate, a microwave, and a toaster oven, each night for dinner Eldon either reheated portions of frozen vegetable soup he had made in advance, or baked lasagna in a loaf pan. To keep the latter interesting, he tried making it with all sorts of different ingredients, like substituting cream cheese for the ricotta.

A walk-in closet originally designed for art-supply storage was repurposed for my bedroom. Eldon moved all the stored supplies into his own room, including the screen printer he'd used to design T-shirts long ago as well as Alan's vast array of paints, colored pencils, and pastels which he still regularly used to create fantastical, creepy science fiction scenes with monsters and aliens. Next, my uncle built a wide enough shelf along one wall to support a twin-size mattress. Aside from that there was only a desk and chair in the room. I had to rely on a single, bare light bulb installed overhead for illumination as there was no window. Alan lived in one of the legitimate bedrooms, and while Eldon had offered me the other, it didn't feel right as a freeloader to take it. Besides, I didn't have anything more than clothing with me there, so the walk-in closet suited my needs just fine.

The stair-covering that Eldon had put in place could be slid aside allowing Alan and me to move freely between the two territories. My cousin didn't play favorites, despite choosing to reside in his father's section of the house. He never talked about his feelings, and when in the presence of one parent, he never gossiped about the other.

I jumped at any opportunity to watch TV in Arlene's living room, as Eldon didn't keep one upstairs. Most of the time, my aunt was there, and occasionally, Alan. Sometimes I'd convince them to watch a comedy on Turner Classic Movies, like *The Court Jester* or *The Secret Life of Walter Mitty*. Desperate for anything remotely humorous and light-hearted, I'd slap my knee and laugh until tears streamed down my face. Arlene and Alan, eyes wide, would both stare at me like I was insane.

One evening when I went downstairs and asked my aunt if I could join her, she gave me a hard look. "Yes," she said, slowly drawing out the word. "But not if you're here just to watch TV." Her dark brown eyes held mine in an intense gaze.

I dropped awkwardly onto the couch next to her, avoiding eye contact while commanding my brain to produce a convincing response. Several seconds of painful silence passed with Arlene continuing to stare at me. "So," I blurted, "how's the teaching job going?" I turned to face my aunt, whose knitted brow told me she knew darn well I wasn't there for anything other than the TV.

"Good," she said, after a long pause.

Arlene wasn't physically affectionate with me, her son, or anyone so far as I'd ever seen. It was hard to believe she was a teacher at a local elementary school. Perhaps she was softer at work. Then again, her demeanor was likely conducive to keeping unruly children in line.

Just what does she think is going on here? I wondered. I was a sad, lonely teenager with very little to keep myself entertained. Why did she have to begrudge me the one nonschool activity that brought me some blessed relief from the dark thoughts and anguish I felt after spending so much time alone in my room? I forced myself to continue conversing with her, and after about ten minutes, she seemed to let her guard down as she resumed working with her ball of yarn and watching her program. I stuck around for another hour, just to make sure things were all right between us.

After that, I took to sneaking downstairs on the evenings that my aunt didn't return home until after dark. I would watch TV and steal snacks from her kitchen, hoping to God she didn't count the number of chocolate bars she purchased by the box and kept in her refrigerator. The second I saw her headlights illuminate the driveway, I'd shut off the TV and race back upstairs to my room.

Ironically, it was Arlene I decided to ask about how you know when you're in love. Her eyes took on a distant look. "Oh, you just know," she said softly, as her fingers caressed the collar of her ivory silk blouse. "Your heart will tell you." I wondered whether she was thinking of her courtship with Eldon—if she could even recall a day when they'd had feelings for each other. Perhaps she was picturing Elvis, of whom she had several framed photos from his early films and concerts displayed throughout her kitchen and dining room. I would never know who had lit up that sparkle in her eye, but I was certain it felt amazing to be in love.

I could talk with Eldon about anything in the entire world. No topic was off limits, with one exception: he didn't want to hear a bad word about his brother and refused to engage if I said anything about the downfall of my relationship with Dad.

I never cared for my cousin, especially given he wasn't welcoming to me in the slightest while I lived there. He displayed few emotions other than occasional exasperation and anger. Now that he was a teenager, his differences were even more pronounced as he didn't have close friends or participate in social activities. Yet he made comments that indicated he thought very highly of himself and his artistic abilities.

Upon noticing a chipmunk pelt on Alan's bookshelf, I pointed in horror at the miniature animal-skin rug. "Is that real?" I asked.

He explained how he had removed it himself from roadkill.

"Ew," I said.

"I said it was dead already!" he snapped.

I pictured him skinning a tiny flattened rodent. *How did he even have the right tools for that sort of a task?* I wondered.

Whenever my siblings and I used to hug Eldon as children, Alan would throw a temper tantrum. He didn't like sharing his father with us, which I found odd considering that he himself never initiated contact with his father. I was relieved that this no longer seemed to be an issue, given that I hugged Eldon at the end of each day. I felt immensely fortunate to have him in my life.

Chapter 75

When the weather was good, I took long walks up the quiet road leading past a golf course on one side and colonial houses on the other. I always brought a plastic bag to pick up litter along the side of the road, since Satmardeva taught students to leave a place cleaner than you found it. I also returned to my old habit of smoking, having learned that the young clerk at the convenience store a short walk down the road would sell cigarettes to minors. Fortunately, she seemed more interested in doing me a favor as a friend than upholding the law.

Skirting along the river behind Eldon's house, I'd explore the vast acres of woods for hours at a time, sit down to smoke amongst the silent congregation of birch trees, and try to derive comfort from nature. Songbirds swept through the area, landing on branches to chirp their secret language to each other. It was strange to think that no matter how bad humans had it during any point in history, the birds above were oblivious. They shared their joy with us, through song, but our concerns weren't their concerns.

I would have preferred spending my free time with friends, of which I had several, but we lived far apart, and none had a car. Plus, I was too embarrassed by the situation at my aunt and uncle's house to invite anyone there.

I spent a great deal of time in my room as well, doing homework, writing in my diary, and making tiny figures and beads out of clay, which I would harden in the toaster oven like it was a kiln. I consumed chocolate daily, easily putting away a pound of candy before the week was up. Whenever

Eldon was going to the grocery store and he asked if I had any requests, I responded, "Chocolate!"

Once when I stayed home from school with the flu, I sat on the bare wood living room floor in my pajamas, legs splayed out in front of me, exhausted from vomiting all morning. My need for the comfort that sugar brought me was so strong that, after determining I'd thoroughly emptied the contents of my stomach, I rinsed out my mouth and proceeded to eat handful after handful of M&Ms.

During this period, I felt especially spiritually connected. I held one-way conversations with my guru in my head, thanking him for the good things I had in my life and praying for my family. I sang bhajans in my room and accompanied Eldon to Sunday services each week. My aunt no longer attended, and Alan's presence was inconsistent. I would cheerfully link my arm through my uncle's as we walked from the parking lot to the worship hall. It was the closest I'd come to recapturing the childhood happiness that had been eluding me for so long. Each time, I found myself searching the crowd for my parents. Their absence was palpable, like negative space on a canvas.

Because of the bakery, my mother and father had been pillars of the community, regardless of the fact that neither had sought the spotlight. People who had known my parents would ask about them. The conversation played out the same way every time, like a script.

Person: "How are your parents doing?"

Me, with a forced smile: "Good. Really good."

Person: "Is your dad still baking?"

Me, with a forced chuckle: "No, he went into childcare."

Person: "Oh, that's too bad. His bread was the best I ever ate."

I loathed being forced to serve as my family's mouthpiece. Ashamed to confess that my parents had split up, I felt compelled to pretend everything was fine. Being in such a small community meant living under a microscope, and I didn't want that which pained me most in the world to become fodder for local gossip. Thus, the truth remained a secret.

My faith was stronger than ever, which helped give me strength, but it didn't change the fact that I was terribly lonely, and spending so much time in introspection perpetuated the solitary existence. Occasionally I would jolt awake late in the night, scanning the darkness in terror, wondering where I was. I pored over photos from childhood in the album I'd asked Karina to ship me and constantly worried about my siblings' welfare since they were still stuck living with my parents.

I asked Eldon, "What do you think heaven is like?"

"I think it's exactly what you want it to be," he said, with conviction.

I liked the sound of that.

"So it could be a big playground in the sky?" I asked, cracking a goofy smile to mask the fact that I actually took the topic quite seriously. I earnestly wanted to know what to expect in the afterlife.

"Sure," Eldon said, with a chuckle.

I envisioned my family sitting around our old wooden dining table, smiling and laughing as we talked. Heaven would surely reunite us, I decided.

Chapter 76

Though founded on our guru's teachings, Satmardeva School was open to all, not just those who practiced our faith, promoting personal development and selfless service in addition to academic achievement.

It was a small, humble institution with fewer than 150 students from kindergarten through twelfth grade. We addressed our teachers by their first names, brought our own lunches since there was no cafeteria, and removed our shoes when entering any of the individual buildings spread across the campus. Such a great number of students attended on partial or full scholarships that the school couldn't afford a janitor. Instead, they maintained an annual cleaning schedule where every parent was responsible for cleaning a section of the school on rotation.

The campus was so vast that students got to go sledding on the hillside in winter, after which we would be treated to hot chocolate and freshly made popcorn. Maple trees were tapped in the spring, and the syrup boiled right on the property, giving students an exciting up-close look at the process from start to finish. There were no bullies at the school, and students enjoyed competing for the highest grades and best time on cross-country team runs.

On the first day of school, I was nervous about boarding the bus and seeing other students my age who would remember my family's departure. I hadn't made it through Satmardeva continuously for all grades, as many others had, and perhaps it looked like I'd come crawling back because I couldn't hack it in public school. However, the students I'd known from before showed genuine curiosity about where I'd been for the past few years and how my family was doing. As with my parents' peers, I simply told them everyone was doing well.

Monday through Friday I felt a sustained gratefulness for being able to reconnect with old friends and make new ones and learn from remarkably invested, caring teachers in the dynamic, enriching environment at Satmardeva. I was surely the jolliest student ever to walk the campus; during school hours I had everything I needed in the healthiest atmosphere I'd known in a long time. Outside of school, however, when I was alone again, dark thoughts crept back into my head, and I missed my siblings terribly.

Though I had returned to my hometown, I didn't feel I truly belonged because I was the only student living without my family, burdened by an unusual set of concerns that no high schooler should have. While my friends navigated the emotional ups and downs of developing feelings for a boy, suffering unrequited love, and dating, I was preoccupied with the emotional repercussions of a bleak financial situation and being without my family.

On weekends, as arranged, I reported to the main floor of the high school building to clean. With no one serving as a monitor, I had the flexibility to arrive when I wanted and move at my own pace as I swept and mopped the classrooms—which were often littered with tiny paper balls that boys would throw at each other during the week—vacuumed the carpeted hallway and library, cleaned the bathrooms, and took out the garbage. I occasionally volunteered to cover other people's shifts as well, as the going rate for the service was fifty dollars, the largest sum of money I could make at one time.

I yearned to participate in extracurricular activities as most other students did, like playing an instrument or sports. Most of my friends were either on the soccer or field hockey teams. Unable to afford the upfront cost of cleats and a uniform meant I couldn't join the soccer team. Hopeful I could come up with the weekly payments for guitar lessons, I started learning from a freelance music teacher on campus and would practice scales and chords at home on a guitar he loaned me. I was only able to continue lessons for a couple of months before my meager savings ran out. I turned to participating in free activities, playing a bit role as the ghost of Cinderella's mother in *Into the Woods* and singing in the school chorus.

Having attended multiple schools, primarily alternative ones at that, I was behind academically. Satmardeva staff determined I was two grades behind, specifically, and thus most of my classes were with younger students. I enjoyed the majority of my classes and earned high grades in everything except algebra and biology. In my free time I read the classics I had missed, borrowing such titles as *Catcher in the Rye* and *Catch-22* off my cousin's bookshelf.

Lacking the funds to purchase what I might really want to wear, I didn't have the luxury of crafting a personal style. I had a few staples, like blue jeans and a burgundy wool cardigan that I was partial to, plus Converse sneakers and Doc Marten boots. I gave the wrong impression about myself when Arlene thoughtfully took me back-to-school shopping at TJ Maxx, where I selected a series of T-shirts featuring the Tasmanian Devil from *Looney Toons* standing next to a Harley Davidson. I was hoping I could pass them off as an ironic fashion statement. However, a student in my Spanish class asked, "Are you, like, really into motorcycles?" I said "Huh?" taken aback by a question that seemed to come out of left field. The boy silently pointed at the shirt I was wearing. "Oh! No," I said, and felt myself blush. Most days I wore T-shirts promoting vitamin brands, freebies Mom got from the health food store where she worked.

The school received a monthly delivery of a free newspaper comprised of editorial pieces and album reviews submitted by teenagers across the Northeast. In payment for a published article, authors would receive a twenty-dollar gift certificate to a leading music store chain. The paper had a pen pal section, which caught my eye. As a young child I had gotten the opportunity to write to Diana, a girl my age in South Dakota, when my entire class swapped letters with her class. It was exciting to meet someone so far away and hear about how her day-to-day life differed from my own. This new opportunity to make a pen pal appealed to me because I had a lot of free time on my hands when I wasn't at school. I found myself intrigued by Kai's short blurb about himself, despite it containing references to bands with which I wasn't familiar. But the last line made me giggle: "P.S. – I'm allergic to bees," he had written. The inclusion of this random factoid indicated to me that Kai had a great sense of humor, so I wrote to him. To my delight, he wrote back a lengthy, well-composed letter. We struck up a friendship, regularly exchanging multipage letters, mine destined for the Philadelphia suburbs and his reaching me all the way in rural Vermont. I looked forward to his letters with great anticipation, hungry for a friendship I could maintain outside of school hours.

Chapter 77

Karina called, saying she had bad news.

"What happened?" I asked warily.

"I came home from work today," she said, "to find that Dad had taken Teddy to the pet store."

"What are you talking about?" I asked, clutching the phone handset tightly in both hands.

"He gave Teddy away to the pet store down the street," she said.

"Well, go to the store and get him back!" I implored.

"I tried, Ang," Karina said. "I went down there right away and asked about a beige rat that would have just been brought in. They said he was already gone."

"Gone?! Gone?!" I shouted as I started sobbing. "Where the hell did he go? Did they have any details?"

"No, they didn't know," she said softly. "He's gone, Angie. I'm so sorry."

She feared I would blame her, since Teddy was under her care. But it wasn't her fault. It was my fault. I was the one who chose to move back to Vermont. In order to get off the sinking ship, I had abandoned my best friend, just as I had my siblings. Now I was paying the price for my freedom.

I couldn't accept that Dad would have taken it upon himself to carry out such an act. It didn't make any sense—he kept creatures in cages for his preschoolers; why would he get rid of my pet? If anything, he could have placed Teddy's cage in the living room with the other creatures, for the children's amusement. There could only be one reason he would behave so callously, specifically when there was no one present at the time to protect my interests: it had to have been Maude's influence. My father had been right by my side when I purchased Teddy and over the following weeks had witnessed my rapidly developing affection for my new friend. While he likely couldn't comprehend how deeply attached I was to Teddy, even a child's minimal fondness for a pet would warrant a parent checking first about whether or not it was okay to give the pet away.

After getting off the phone, I curled up into the fetal position and rocked myself back and forth on my bed as I wept into my pillow. I wouldn't confront Dad about it. Experience had taught me that I couldn't share my frustration or disappointment, as it only resulted in my parents withholding love from me. Nothing would bring Teddy back. Had I really thought that life would be put on hold in Washington while I stepped away to finish high school, returning with diploma in hand to find everything as it had been left?

Even though my parents hadn't physically died, I grieved their loss all the same because the people I'd known them to be for the first twelve years of my life were gone. It would have been better if they had actually passed away so I could mourn the death of loving parents rather than bitterly resent the strangers they'd become.

It had taken so little for them to be pushed over the edge, leaving neither of them wanting responsibility for their children after the marriage dissolved. I couldn't help but wonder what had held things together as my parents built their family in Vermont. Perhaps it had merely been the distraction of bringing another unplanned child into the world every few years.

My heart ached as I thought about how all that had been lost could never be regained. The only thing I knew about this mysterious turn of events was that those parents I'd had, pre-separation, wouldn't have carelessly allowed our childhood innocence, the tight-knit family, the heirlooms with sentimental value, and now my beloved pet rat to slip away into the ether. Every element of our once special way of life had systematically been dismantled. Everything my parents had taught us about right from wrong, based on the principles of our faith, was tossed aside once no longer convenient. Although my mother's lifestyle changes were shocking and disturbing, the real betrayal for me was dealt by my father. He had been my world; I relied on him and trusted him, but he had only loved me in the contentment of my youth or when I held my tongue. Once I developed a mind of my own and opinions that differed from his, he lost interest. He had allowed Maude to isolate him, and rather than absence making the heart grow fonder, it must have magnified the echoes of our hurtful words from when my siblings and I chastised him for how he had handled the separation.

After returning to Heathburn, I found myself once again in those sacred places so steeped in family history that the air nearly vibrated. With all my heart I yearned for everything to be as I'd known it before.

I was left with a wrenching sensation in my chest as I walked along the dirt road to the worship hall without my father and as I peered at my old home now occupied by another family. The house looked entirely different and didn't have the same spark. The new owners had torn down the standalone garage my parents had constructed after they'd converted the basement's built-in garage into the bakery. With the old garage restored, all semblance of the bakery was long gone, and the downstairs was a proper basement, I imagined. They had also painted over the stately gray-brown shade my mother had painstakingly selected with a brick red.

Now my bus stop was directly across the road from the house, so each and every weekday morning while I waited for the bus, I stood staring at my childhood home. And after I was dropped off in the afternoon, I'd see it once again. Twice a day, five days a week, I gazed at that empty shell of a house that should still have had my family warmly installed inside, not some strangers who didn't even recognize how special it was. I was back, but I couldn't recover what had been lost no matter how badly I yearned for it.

The memory of walking with my father to the worship hall played and replayed in my head like a fever dream. I was still living it, and yet I wasn't. The ghosts of happy memories were my constant companion and greatest torment.

Between the two of them, my parents had created an ocean of disappointment that sent wave after wave crashing over me when I'd hardly had time to right myself after the last toppling. I couldn't stop comparing then and now, how stark a contrast our lives were. *How did it come to this? How did it come to this?* I asked the universe, as I rocked back and forth on my bed.

Chapter 78

I came home from school one afternoon to find Eldon sitting at the kitchen table with his brows furrowed. Alan had stayed after school to practice with the track team, so I knew whatever appeared to be troubling my uncle was coming my way.

"We need to talk," he said gloomily, beckoning to a nearby chair. I set my backpack on the floor, removed my shoes, and moved silently to take a seat.

"Well," he said, drawing in a sharp breath and looking at the floor, "Clark called me in for a meeting this afternoon."

Why would my principal want to meet with Eldon? My mind was already racing, searching for an answer. My grades were high, my school conduct and attendance inscrutable; there was no conceivable reason for an unexpected parent-teacher conference between the two of them.

"He said he's aware of my marital issues," Eldon said, shifting in his chair. He paused, raised his upturned palms, and then let his hands drop back into his lap.

I wondered whether Arlene herself had advised school officials or whether it was the deed of a busybody from within the community. I doubted very much that Alan, antisocial and unsentimental as he was, would have shared a single detail with anyone about his home life. I collected my thoughts in preparation to assure my uncle that no one had heard it from me. He met my gaze briefly, then shifted his eyes back to the floor. "He has concerns about the nature of our relationship," he finished, beckoning between the two of us.

The collar of my wool flannel shirt prickled uncomfortably against the back of my neck. "What was he basing this on?" I asked, afraid of the answer.

"Specifically, he mentioned seeing us walk to the worship hall arm in arm and sitting too close during services."

"*What?*" I said, shaking my head. "What's Clark doing monitoring our behavior during Sunday services?"

Not only was this an excruciatingly uncomfortable topic, but there was also the absurdity of Clark's having acted on suspicion without due diligence. Living with Eldon had been like getting a second chance with my own father, since they were so similar in appearance and mannerisms. I had cherished having a close relative host me, to make the separation from my family a little less painful.

What Clark didn't bother to find out before making this vile accusation was that I used to walk to the worship hall with my arm linked through my father's. And I didn't sit any closer to Eldon than any person sat next to their kin. Further, I was regularly meeting after school with our congregation's leader Randall for emotional support, and had he been consulted, he would have quickly dispelled Clark's concerns.

"So what do we do about this?" I asked, swallowing the lump in my throat.

Eldon gently raised a hand in the air as though to stay me.

"We shouldn't have any more physical contact," he said softly, "and I would ask that you don't sit so close to me at Sunday services."

I dropped my head and hunched forward as the gravity of what he was saying sunk in. The pit in my stomach told me I would never feel at ease around my uncle again. It was now incumbent on me, a child, to remain vigilant about how my conduct could be interpreted by others.

In one thoughtless act, my principal had robbed me of the only source of physical contact I had and ruined something pure. I felt ashamed both of my need for physical contact and that Eldon had never been the one to initiate it.

I pictured Clark, with his curly black hair, pockmarked cheeks, and wire-rimmed glasses, staring at me from across his desk with a pursed mouth after I burst into his office to set the record straight. I would rant about how first I'd lost my family, and now I'd lost my surrogate parent thanks to him sticking his nose in our business. But angry as I was, I couldn't have a showdown with the principal; I'd be expelled for such behavior. Instead, I would have to simply respect Eldon's wishes and modify my behavior.

Chapter 79

After getting off the bus one afternoon, I noticed from the road that all the young pine trees Eldon had planted in a row at the edge of their property had been hacked down. All six of them lay fallen in his yard, beside their stumps. As I entered the driveway, it was apparent that the side of the house had sustained damage too. I felt a little frightened. It was the only time I ever wished Alan were with me, but he was at track practice.

I found Eldon sitting in his room reading and asked what had happened. He looked up from his book and, with a glint of madness in his eyes, explained that Arlene had been continuing to use his garden, despite his repeated warnings that he'd planted it and tended to it and would be the only one to benefit from it. When he noticed indications that Arlene was continuing to harvest vegetables, he destroyed the entire garden. Then he'd gone on to chop down the saplings by the road that were supposed to form a privacy barrier as they grew larger. Finally, he had smashed the side of the house with a shovel. I mumbled something about it being unfair of Arlene to use his garden, and quickly retreated to my bedroom.

Over the months, as those saplings continued to lay in a heap on the lawn and the sheet rock continued to peek out from the crumbling corner of the house with nothing being done to fix the violence that had occurred, it was a constant reminder that things weren't well in this home.

When I asked Mom over the phone why Eldon and Arlene didn't simply get divorced, she said that while my uncle had built the house from the foundation up, it was my aunt who financed it. Thus, neither was willing to part with the property.

"But why did they get married in the first place?" I asked. "They don't even like each other."

Mom explained that long before my time, Eldon had been deeply in love with a different woman, Arlene's best friend, who tragically passed away from cancer. After she died, Eldon left California where he'd been living with her. Arlene, having decided she had feelings for him, followed Eldon all the way to the East Coast. As impossible as it was to imagine now, she wouldn't give up until he married her.

Why all that effort just to end up locked in this state of perpetual misery?

When Eldon suddenly stopped speaking to me as well, I assumed it was because I had become too much of a burden. After a couple weeks passed with him still avoiding me, I spoke with Judy, Satmardeva's admissions counselor, about finding a different host family to live with.

One afternoon as Eldon and I drove to the library, I asked why he had stopped speaking to me.

"Okay," he said slowly. "Why don't we go for a walk and talk about it?"

We entered the park next to the library and strolled past a small pond where Dad used to take my siblings and me to feed ducks as a child. It was a mild, sunny afternoon. Eldon clasped his hands behind his back as he walked. From afar we probably looked like we were engaged in pleasant conversation.

"I feel you have been increasingly critical of me," my uncle said. "Your comments are judgmental, and it makes it uncomfortable to be around you." His gaze remained on the path ahead.

The heat rose in my cheeks. I couldn't believe what I was hearing. He didn't have even one specific example for me; he simply kept reiterating the accusation. I was unable to recall anything in my behavior that would have come across as judgmental of him. I had certainly made comments that were critical of my parents, but I knew in my heart I had never done so against him. I didn't harbor a single negative feeling about Eldon. While I wished he didn't have to live his life in a depressed state, I didn't think any less of him for it.

In my eyes, Eldon had saved me from a dead-end home life in Washington. He was my beloved surrogate father. It was distressing to learn that he was unaware of the fact I held him in such high regard. As I listened to him explain how he perceived my demeanor, I realized with horror that he was painting a picture of Arlene. How could I possibly tell my uncle he had me confused with his estranged wife?

"I'm sorry if I've made you feel that way," I said. My tongue felt heavy and knocked against the roof of my mouth stiffly as though forming words for the first time. "I don't recall saying anything judgmental, and if I ever did, I certainly didn't mean it that way."

I glanced back toward Eldon's van, parked just up the street across from the library. It was astounding to think that a decade earlier I had spent time in the children's area of that very same library admiring a Victorian dollhouse while Dad picked out books to read to us kids at home. I thought about how much simpler life was back then, not having to navigate the emotional turmoil that characterized adults' lives.

I was struck with the full weight of the realization that Arlene had been right all along. Wishing to flee to the safety of the van so I could cry in private, I considered how I had initially thought my aunt selfish and unkind for cautioning me not to move into their house eight months earlier.

Chapter 80

Mom had moved an hour-and-a-half drive south of Bellevue to live with her long-term boyfriend, Winston. Karina, Heidi, and Ryan went with her, while Ben returned to Dad's house.

One weekend a month Karina had to report to the nearest military base as part of being in the reserves. She wrote to me about meeting up with an old acquaintance named Rick when he came to Seattle from his station in Alaska to do his exit papers; he had been discharged from the military for instigating a physical altercation with a superior. Karina and Rick had met in boot camp and, at this second chance meeting, started dating.

Rick joined Karina at Winston's house. Struggling financially, they stole some items from Winston, including a stereo that they sold at a pawn shop. I knew it had to have been Rick's influence. This wasn't the sister I knew; she had never stolen anything in her life.

When Mom discovered what they'd done, she kicked them out. They decided to move to Houston where Rick was originally from. For a couple months they lived in a cramped apartment. With Karina unemployed and Rick making minimum wage at a pizza shop, the only full meal they had each day was the free pizza Rick was permitted to take home after his shift. I worried about my sister and wished she had stayed at Winston's house.

Chapter 81

When eleventh grade concluded, Satmardeva's special fund for underprivileged students enabled me to fly back to Washington for the summer. I joined Mom and my siblings at Winston's quaint, old-fashioned house, which was located in a calm little pocket of Americana with the potential to resuscitate any dysfunctional family. All the homes in his slow-paced suburban neighborhood were molded from the same cookie cutter, each with an enclosed porch and bay windows on the second floor overlooking the street.

I found that Mom had adopted another black cat from the humane society, which she named Zima after the carbonated alcoholic beverage that had become her new favorite. Mom only drank one bottle at a time, just enough to prove that she was an adult who could do anything she wanted. Like a child wobbling around unsteadily while playing dress-up in her mother's high heels, there was an awkwardness to Mom's alcohol consumption stemming from her late start.

"Why is the radio on in an empty kitchen?" I asked Mom as I came down from the attic.

"It's for the kombucha mushroom," she said, looking up from the magazine she was reading at the dining room table. "The bacteria colonies respond well to classical music."

I ducked inside the pantry and spotted an enormous glass jar in which kombucha was fermenting, suspended in dark tea. It was a nasty looking substance that Mom declared would bestow health and vitality. *Well, that's interesting,* I thought. *She cares more about a mushroom's well-being than she did about mine when I lived with her.*

∽

One afternoon, Mom, Ryan, and I were having lunch in Winston's dining room.

"Well, the divorce was finalized today," my mother said, sighing.

I looked up from my sandwich.

"Eighteen years of marriage, over," she said, tears springing to her eyes.

"Oh," I said, feeling obligated to acknowledge her statement.

My little brother was thumbing through a comic book. He remained quiet as though disinterested, or perhaps it was simply above his head. I had thought the divorce was already finalized a long time ago, what with two years having passed since my parents had separated, and them both moving on to different relationships. I felt no sympathy for her, even as she dabbed at her eyes, given that she was the one to end the marriage. I no longer tried to consider things from her perspective and whether her reasons may have been valid. All I knew was that she'd pulled the rip cord that destroyed our family, and the never-ending fallout from that was emotionally exhausting.

Chapter 82

From Houston, Karina described to me in letters how she spent a lot of her time sitting on a swing at a playground near her apartment complex, pondering her future. She was frustrated at her boyfriend Rick's regular use of marijuana and lack of ambition. Her health rapidly declined, between being anemic and going without regular meals. She decided to break up with Rick and return to Washington after learning she was pregnant with Rick's child. She also decided not to tell him about her condition as she didn't feel he would be a good father and he wasn't in a position to provide child support. At the age of twenty, she was prepared to carry her pregnancy to full term despite not having any support.

When Karina returned to Washington from Texas, she was unwelcome at Winston's house since she'd stolen from him. She had no other option than to move back into Ben's old room at Dad's house.

Karina called me, saying she had bad news.

"What is it?" I asked.

"Dad married Maude."

"What?" I buckled over, feeling as though I had just gotten the wind knocked out of me. "How do you know?"

"I noticed that Dad is suddenly wearing some ugly gold ring," Karina said.

"What? When?" I sputtered.

"They got married at city hall, apparently."

I didn't understand why my sister sounded indifferent about the matter. She was probably chewing on her fingernails at that very moment, which she seemed to do when she was bored rather than stressed. "Did anyone know about it before it happened? Did anyone attend?" I asked.

"I don't think so," she said. "Dad doesn't even like gold. It's this tacky, wide band with some kind of design on it. They got matching rings—can you believe it?"

I tuned Karina out as my mind started racing through all the implications of this most unwelcome news. There was no longer any shred of hope for my parents' reconciliation; this was the final nail in the coffin. Suddenly a woman I barely knew and didn't want in my life shared our last name. And while I knew my relationship with my father was spoiled, I still found it hard to swallow that he didn't have the decency to tell me he'd gotten remarried.

It was already unbearable enough to go to Dad's house since he'd given Teddy away, a topic I didn't have the courage to address with him. I would be forced to see Dad, however, in order to visit with Karina. I had Mom drop Heidi and me off to stay the weekend. My little sister and I exchanged stiff hugs with Dad and obligatorily greeted Maude. Dad asked me how school was going, and I said good. It was my first time seeing his new wedding ring, which featured a lumpy, knotted design in the middle. He had never worn gold in his life. I knew this meant Maude had picked the set. I noticed he kept switching the ring between two different fingers, as though it were uncomfortable. He caught me looking at it.

"Do you like it?" he asked.

"No," I said.

"Ha!" It was a forced laugh. He didn't know how else to react, I supposed.

Karina told me she hadn't been feeling well, which sounded normal considering she was in her first trimester. On a sunny afternoon, my sisters and I decided to walk a mile to the grocery store to pick up food for ourselves, since Dad didn't keep real food in his kitchen. We maintained a slow gait for Karina's sake, chatting along the way. Once we had picked up a loaf of bread, peanut butter, and jelly, and Karina was wheeling our shopping cart toward the checkout line, things went sideways.

"Ang!" she said, weakly. "I'm going to pass out. Catch me!"

I looked over at her, and before I'd even had time to process the meaning of her words, she had already dropped like a sack of potatoes. Her right arm got lodged between the handle and the cart so that as her legs gave out, she was left hanging from her armpit. The store disappeared, and I looked down at my older sister through a black tunnel.

"Oh my God! Karina! Are you okay?" I called from the other end of the tunnel. My arms flailed helplessly at my sides. I knew I couldn't lift her by myself. All I could do was stare down at her pitifully.

A man stepped forward from another checkout lane and calmly identified himself as a doctor. He gently pulled Karina's arm free from the cart and laid her flat on her back.

"She's pregnant!" I said, by way of explanation.

The man responded that it was likely the anemia that caused Karina to faint.

"Heidi!" I said urgently. "Here's a quarter. Go call Dad!" She looked at me with wide eyes, then dashed out of the store to the nearby pay phone.

Karina started to regain consciousness, blinking slowly and looking around with confusion. I thanked the doctor for his assistance as we helped my sister to her feet. Heidi returned, saying that Dad was on his way to pick us up. We rang up our purchases and, with each of us supporting Karina on one side, walked her out of the store. Still shaky, she insisted that she didn't want medical attention.

Dad pulled up shortly, staying put in the driver's seat. Heidi and I gently maneuvered Karina into the back seat, sitting on either side of her.

"Karina fainted in the store," I said.

"Is she all right?" Dad asked, glancing in the rearview mirror.

"Yeah, I'm okay," Karina said stoically. I looked at her pale face. She stared straight ahead, with her eyebrows pinched together.

Dad said nothing more as he drove us back to his house, whereupon he retreated to his room and closed the door behind him.

Even though I felt terrible that Karina had to stay somewhere with so little support or concern for her state of being, I couldn't remain at Dad's house with her. It was more than I could bear to be in that tense environment, so Heidi and I returned to Winston's house to stay with Mom.

Chapter 83

My pen pal Kai continued sending letters throughout the summer by way of Winston's post office box. I would coerce Heidi into walking a few blocks downtown with me each day to check the mail. In payment for her accompaniment, I would buy us ice cream sandwiches or candy bars from the convenience store, often with the help of change I'd scrounged together from Winston's couch cushions.

Whenever I received correspondence, I would hoot with joy. Heidi, being twelve, would roll her eyes. We'd sit in the grass at a small park near the post office to eat our treats while I read the latest letter out loud. Kai and I wrote to each other about our everyday challenges, our mutual fascination for wildlife, and our hopes for the future. They were long letters, often twelve to twenty pages in length. We'd illustrate the envelopes, making the receipt of a letter even more exciting.

Kai sent me a photo of himself hanging upside down from a tree in his backyard. I found him utterly charming in his baseball cap, red-and-white flannel, and camouflage shorts. I kept the photo tucked into the frame of the mirror that hung in the attic and blushed every time I looked at it. I had never seen anyone so handsome. Having fallen in love with him, I yearned to meet Kai in person.

Much to my surprise, Winston ended up being my favorite of all Mom's suitors. I harbored guilt for having been paid off to be polite when I met him. Though only in his late forties, his lingering Southern accent delivered in rather muffled speech made him sound much older. Hailing from Mississippi, he called his wallet a billfold, which he pronounced as "beel-fold." He said that his friends in high school nicknamed him Bro Pill on account of his large round head that resembled a basketball, which was referred to as a pill where he came from.

Winston was afraid of the dark, according to Mom. She mocked him about it behind his back. But I didn't find his fear the least bit surprising, considering he had served as a paratrooper in the Vietnam War, the source of his facial scar, which proved he'd seen the worst of it. The track that curved the length of his left cheek from the corner of his upper jaw to the edge of his mouth told the tale of how his flesh was sliced clean through by a machete when he was in the jungle. Had it struck an inch higher or lower, he probably would have lost a section of his jaw. Winston had likely witnessed unspeakably terrible acts that would leave anyone afraid of the dark. I never asked what he was doing participating in the atrocities of an unjust war, choosing instead to assume he had been drafted and had no choice. If otherwise, I didn't want to know; I didn't want anything to tarnish my opinion that he was a good guy.

It was hard to believe that Winston had once been a soldier, given his calm, fatherly demeanor. His only remaining connection as a veteran was shopping at the commissary and getting his hair trimmed at the barber shop every two weeks on the nearby military base. While he didn't wear fancy clothes like someone trying to impress, he maintained a respectable appearance in slacks and pressed shirts and by keeping clean-shaven.

I enjoyed mornings in Winston's house, drawn downstairs by the wafting scent of fresh coffee. Making a beeline for the carafe, I'd pour myself a cup and watch the dark liquid turn beige with the addition of hazelnut creamer. Clasping the warm mug in my hands, I felt perfectly content. Being at Winston's made it easy to fall into a false sense of security that we were in a stable household. We were like a real family sitting around the table at breakfast, Winston reading the paper with his bifocals perched near the end of his nose. With elbows propped on the table, I used my raised mug to hide my smirk at how charmingly silly he looked.

For the first time in recent memory, Mom had rules for us. Since Winston never cussed, we were forbidden from cussing. We were to observe proper manners at the table, not watch TV while eating, and contribute to keeping the house clean.

I developed a genuine fondness for Winston as soon as I spent enough time around him to realize he was the real deal. He always showed respect for my mother and humored my younger siblings by chuckling at the ridiculous sentiments he sometimes heard from them. His role as a paratrooper in the Vietnam War and job as a guard at McNeil Prison must have meant he'd seen the worst of humanity, yet still he remained calm, collected, and soft-spoken at all times. All my siblings felt the same as I did about this man who in every way acted like a father to us. I occasionally hugged Winston, just as I did my mother.

"He only wants to hug you so he can feel your breasts pushed up against him," Mom said of this new development.

I was interested in skydiving, and Winston said he could take me as he hadn't forgotten how to jump out of a plane.

"I don't want you to go skydiving with him," Mom told me in private. "He's only offering to take you so that he can feel your body strapped against his."

I didn't really believe Winston would take me skydiving; it was more likely something he said to feel relevant to a teenager. But it was deeply troubling to hear these kinds of statements from my mother, which made me wonder why she would be in a relationship with a man that she suspected had these kinds of motives.

When Victoria's Secret catalogs arrived in the mail for her, Mom hid them so Winston couldn't look at the pictures.

"Don't put your laundry in the family hamper anymore," she said, upon finding me depositing my dirty laundry there. "Wash it separately."

"Why?"

"Because men like to sniff women's panties," she said, "and I don't want Winston having access to yours."

I was appalled to learn of this disgusting phenomenon and, as always, secretly questioned the type of people with whom my mother associated. I didn't for one second believe Winston engaged in such an act, but I scooped my laundry back into my arms if only to keep her off my back.

⌒

One afternoon, I sat reading S.E. Hinton's *The Outsiders* upstairs in the bedroom that I shared with Heidi. Really just a finished attic, it was one long A-frame room that ran the length of the house. It had no door, only a narrow staircase at the far end that led down to the laundry room behind the kitchen. Ryan came up to inform me he was going down the street to play with a friend.

"Winston said I should let you know I'm leaving," he said, already turning to head back down the stairs. It dawned on me that for the first time I would be alone in the house with Winston, given that Mom had taken Heidi to get a haircut.

"Wait, Ryan!" I said, urgently. "If you stay here, I'll give you anything you want. A candy bar, or five dollars."

Mom's warnings about all men being perverts flooded my mind. I didn't have any business being in that house alone with Winston. How did I ever let myself get into such a predicament?

I was unable to convince Ryan to remain. He left to meet with his friend, and the house fell silent. Breaking into a cold sweat, I dropped into a squatted position with my back against the wall, drawing rapid, shallow breaths. I surveyed the bedroom for an escape, should I require one. Then I rocketed up and over to the open bay windows that looked out over the flat porch roof. I'd seen the cat regularly go out the window and walk around on the roof and hoped it would support my weight as well. Clutching the window frame with one hand and chewing on my bottom lip, I craned my neck left and right to survey the landscape. Responsible for protecting myself, I had to make a plan in case Winston came upstairs. With the house being right on the street, I would be safe as long I climbed onto the roof and jumped down into the front yard. At worst I would suffer a broken ankle, but even if I had to lie on the grass shouting for help, I would still be safe.

Gulping repeatedly, I attempted to swallow my terror. I remained poised at the bay windows, straining to hear any sound that would indicate where Winston was and what he was doing. However, the house remained as still and quiet as if I were there alone. Winston never came up and didn't so much as call up the stairs to interact with me.

When Mom returned home with Heidi an hour later, my anxiety abated. In all likelihood, Winston had spent the entire time in the living room reading the paper behind his bifocals. I felt ashamed for thinking such rotten things about him and never told anyone about having gotten so worked up over nothing.

As summer drew to a close, I talked with Eldon on the phone. He sounded surprisingly upbeat and said he was looking forward to seeing me. We arranged for him to pick me up from Logan Airport in Boston when I flew back in a couple weeks. Because our conversation was flowing so smoothly, I confessed to him how I'd approached Judy about finding another host family due to my concern that I was a financial burden on him. Now that the air had been cleared between us and he had confirmed it was fine for me to stay on with him, I would tell Judy to disregard my request. Upon hearing this, Eldon's tone suddenly changed. I wasn't sure what to make of it.

On the day Mom was to take me to the airport so that I could return to Vermont for my senior year, out of nowhere she insisted that I needed a new sports bra. She wanted to stop at a department store on the way to get me one. I told her I didn't want to worry about that right now; I just wanted to get to the airport with plenty of time to spare before my flight. Despite the fact that I'd flown a few times now, the whole process still made me anxious—making my way through an airport, trying to find the right gate in a very finite amount of time. Mom stopped anyway. It took a while selecting and trying on bras, and as I kept checking the time, I randomly selected one, insisting it was the one to purchase.

As we neared the airport, Mom got lost, and driving around in circles, she started cussing while my stomach tightened into knots. We stopped at a gas station, and I ran in to get directions, which I could hardly process and was fearful I wouldn't retain. The man told us to head back in the opposite direction and that we couldn't miss the signs so long as we were on the highway.

"It was way back the way we just came!" I said tersely, as I slipped into the passenger seat. I felt upset at my mother for waiting until the last minute to take me clothes shopping.

Mom screeched to a halt at my airline's terminal, and there was no time for long goodbyes. She was frazzled by this point, and I was irritated and anxious, so I gave her a quick side hug inside the car, hurled myself out the door with my belongings, and began the mad dash to my gate. I made it just before they closed the door. It wasn't flying that frightened me; it was getting to the airport on time and finding my way to the gate through an enormous, crowded place all by myself.

Chapter 84

When I met Eldon in the baggage claim area, he didn't look happy to see me.

"How was your trip?" he asked, in a serious tone that immediately put me on edge.

"It was good," I said. "Thanks for picking me up."

"You're welcome," he said, taking the suitcase from my hand and leading us outside to his truck. He didn't say another word to me for the entire two-hour drive home. It was excruciating sitting there in silence, not knowing what had gone wrong. I couldn't handle the pressure of asking him what he was upset about this time. I kept my gaze out the window, though it was dark, wishing I was anywhere but in the cabin of that truck. Before we reached his house, I had already decided I couldn't live with him any longer. This was more than any seventeen-year-old could bear, especially after all the drama I had already been subjected to by my parents. The moment Eldon pulled into his driveway, I thanked him again for picking me up and announced that I would be going to my friend Alyssa's house for the night.

"Would you like a ride there?" my uncle asked, as we stood in the entry. His eyes were dark, and his long, narrow face was set in a frown.

"No, thank you," I said. "I'll walk." I couldn't spend even one more minute in that tense atmosphere and made up an excuse that I had already been sitting for too long, between the flight and the drive back.

It was after nine o'clock, and despite the faint glow of moonlight, it was alarmingly dark out given that there were no streetlights along the back roads in Heathburn. After borrowing a flashlight from Eldon and depositing my suitcase in my bedroom, I started up the road with a few necessities in a backpack. The batteries in the penlight were dying, and the weak beam it emitted barely illuminated the pavement two feet in front of me. After a mile or so, the flashlight gave out entirely, and I walked the remaining mile in the suffocating darkness. I was tempted to pick up my pace, but it seemed more dangerous to hurry if I couldn't see what was in front of me. I also didn't want to chance being struck by a car, so I kept as close to the side of the road as possible without risk of losing my footing at the ragged edge of the pavement and tumbling into the ditch. I had known a boy in ninth grade who was struck and killed by a car as he walked home one night; the driver hadn't seen him as she came around a bend in the road.

The comforting chorus of frogs croaking in the distance was the only soundtrack to my journey, aside from my Converse sneakers scuffing on the pavement. It was slow going, and I was on high alert, but because I had traveled that road countless times over the years both by car and on foot, I knew it well. However, once I turned off the paved road onto the adjoining dirt road, the unmistakable sound of a panting animal suddenly alerted me to the fact that I wasn't alone. Out of the corner of my eye, I could make out the movement of a sizable creature barreling toward me. Alarmed, I froze in place and raised my arms protectively across my chest. To my relief, it turned out to be the friendly Husky that lived in one of the houses at that intersection. Alyssa and I had met him many times before, as he liked to greet us whenever we walked past carrying our sacks of candy from the convenience store near my old house. Not knowing his real name, we had nicknamed him King for his regal gait and good manners.

"Oh! King, you scared me!" I said, as he quietly fell in step by my side. I patted his head, wishing I could take him the rest of the way as my protector, but I didn't want him getting lost. "Go home, boy!" I said. "Your parents are going to wonder where you are. Go on home!" He trotted off, and the rest of my walk was uneventful.

Arriving at Alyssa's, I entered the screened-in patio and knocked on the inner door until I succeeded in rousing her attention.

"Angie!" she exclaimed, opening the door. Her blue eyes were wide with concern. "I wasn't expecting you tonight." She craned her neck to peer out into the empty driveway, her thicket of sandy blond curls falling across her shoulders. "Who brought you here?" she asked.

As I explained all that had happened, I broke down crying. Fortunately, her parents were across the road visiting with her aunt and uncle, so we had privacy. I used the black rotary phone in the kitchen to call my mother. As soon as she answered, I cried all the harder. It was her I reached out to for support because Dad wouldn't take my side if I complained to him about his brother's behavior.

"You probably shouldn't live with him anymore," Mom said. "That doesn't sound like a healthy environment."

"But where will I go?" I whimpered. Wishing I could stay on in Alyssa's summer house once she and her parents returned home to Massachusetts, I pictured living all by myself like Pippi Longstocking. The children's book heroine had all kinds of fun living on her own, keeping animals for friends and rolling out cookie dough on the kitchen floor. I would rather be alone than have to try fitting in with host families, where I couldn't expect to be anything other than the odd one out. Unfortunately, not only did I lack the resources necessary to care for myself, having neither funds nor transportation, but the Barrier's summer house wasn't primed to weather the winter. At the end of the season, they would shutter it and lock it down until the next summer.

⚬

When a classmate's mother offered to let me move in with them, I returned to Eldon's house just long enough to clear out my possessions. I told him I was rotating out so that the burden wouldn't be too much for any one family. An awkward goodbye was exchanged, with no hug offered by either of us.

My cousin never spoke to me again. I wondered what, if anything, Eldon had told him about why I moved out.

One morning after Alan boarded the school bus, he abruptly dropped a large grocery bag into my lap without a word as he passed by. I glanced around to see if anyone had witnessed what felt to me like a humiliating interaction, but it didn't seem anyone had. Inside the bag was mail that had been delivered to me at Eldon's address. It was evident that regardless of whether my uncle had informed Alan of our falling out, the disdain I had for my cousin was mutual.

Given how broken Eldon was, I suddenly realized what a profound loss it must have been for him when our family moved away. We were his only relatives in the state, his only friends as far as I was aware. All he had for company was a bitter wife and an odd son. It must have been crushing for him to lose his only lifeline. And now he had lost me again.

⁂

In my new residence, as at my uncle's house, I remained largely confined to my bedroom doing homework, writing in my diary, and singing bhajans.

I loved the days when I could get to the public library. I would head straight to the children's section and search out all the old books Dad used to read to us kids when we were little. Back then, we all fought to be the lucky one who got to sit in his lap, and the rest would gather around on either side. Dad became each character, doing a gruff voice for villains and monsters and a high-pitched voice for women and children. Steven Kellogg and James Stevenson were our favorite authors as kids. These were the books I sought out at the library, thumbing through each one slowly, savoring every word and illustration.

I was fortunate to secure a part-time salesclerk position at a health food store in the town's center, just a couple miles from the house, which meant I was able to purchase my own groceries. My host family and I weren't of the same faith, so it was imperative that I find a source of food I could eat. I stocked up on organic milk and butter, fruit-sweetened jam, and deli slices made from soy and would pack my own lunches to take to school.

Either someone from my host family or the store owner, Miriam, would give me a ride to and from my weekend shifts. Sometimes I walked home, weather permitting, if I didn't have groceries to carry.

Chapter 85

While my siblings and I swapped letters occasionally, phone conversations were rare as long-distance calls were expensive. I yearned to tell them of my experiences living away from my family, how things were going at school, and how weird it was living with other people. At night, I continued praying to my guru. I asked him to give me the strength I needed to carry on, alone.

Fortunately, an older married couple who were part of my spiritual community and lived up the road kindly gave me a ride on Sundays so that I could attend services at the ashram.

Now as I walked along the dirt road to the worship hall alone, I had to endure double the nostalgia, at times finding myself walking alongside Eldon or putting on my shoes right next to him after the service concluded. My heart would race from both fear and hope that he would speak to me, but since he never looked up, he wasn't aware of my presence. I couldn't bring myself to speak up. It felt odd being on this spiritual journey alone when I'd started out surrounded by my parents, my siblings, and Eldon. I felt utterly forsaken, and the wound was opened afresh each Sunday.

Watching my peers in Vermont interact with their parents and siblings, seeing how comfortable everyone was on their own turf, made me feel sad and resentful that I couldn't enjoy the same comforts with my own family. The loneliness was unbearable.

Chapter 86

In March 1995, while I imagined that all other seniors in America were spending their spring break partying, I returned to Washington for two weeks. It was critical to me that I be present when Karina gave birth, as she was due during that very period of time. Now in her third trimester, she was back living with Mom. Tired and unmotivated, she refused my encouragement to go for short walks around the neighborhood.

Karina chose to give birth at home—now a two-bedroom duplex she shared with Mom, Heidi, and Ryan—with a midwife and doula assisting. Though Mom no longer lived with Winston, they were still seeing each other, and he rushed over as soon as he learned that Karina was in labor. His military training must have been triggered, for he remained posted on the doorstep outside the duplex, as if to safeguard all who were within those walls. Mom invited him to make himself comfortable in the living room, but he held his post, never coming inside until Mom alerted him that the baby had arrived.

Mom, the midwife, and the doula were all in Karina's bedroom, coaching her through the home stretch. My sister was standing, nude, with her arms draped around mom and the midwife for support, while the doula nudged me forward just as the baby's head crowned. I recoiled. Though I'd been tasked with taking pictures of the birth, this didn't strike me as an appropriate time to capture the action. I certainly wouldn't want a permanent reminder of what I had just witnessed, nor did I think my sister would either.

The midwife and doula then helped Karina into bed. I was instructed to massage her abdomen vigorously to stimulate the afterbirth. The midwife told me to press hard while she and the assistant took care of other matters such as cleaning the baby, who was blue and slimy. I did as I was told, at first, while my sister lay pale and motionless. But when she began moaning and writhing in protest, I backed off. I didn't have it in me to punish her in this way after the twelve hours of labor she had just been through. Fortunately, the midwife returned and assumed responsibility for the heinous task. Karina continued to moan faintly while I stood over her, not knowing what to do but feeling protective, and Mom watched by my side, holding the swaddled baby.

Later, I was shocked to find Mom cooking scrambled eggs for my sister's first meal. "She needs protein," she said, when I demanded to know what she was doing.

"Why are they even in the house?" I asked sharply. As part of our vegetarian diet, we had never eaten eggs. It didn't compute to see my mother cooking such a thing as though it were perfectly ordinary.

"Winston eats eggs," she said, "so I keep them on hand."

"Well, it's a good thing Winston chooses not to eat meat, or else that'd be in our fridge too!" I exclaimed, before storming out of the kitchen.

I realized this was her house where she could do as she pleased, but it chafed to have been raised to believe that certain lifestyle choices were the right ones while others were not, with all evidence now pointing to Mom living by the latter. She couldn't just change that which had made us weird outsiders as children when the rules became inconvenient for her.

The irony was infuriating, especially when I recalled the time Mom had brought Karina along to pick me up from Montessori school when I was six. My then nine-year-old sister was sitting in the passenger seat of the van. As Mom pulled onto the road to head for home, I leaned forward between their seats with my pink-and-blue stained hand outstretched. Cupped in my palm was the hardboiled egg I'd painted in class.

"Look what I made!" I said. It was my first time painting an Easter egg.

Karina instantly snatched the offending object from my hand. "We don't eat eggs!" she exclaimed, tossing my art project out of the window.

"Mom!" I protested. "That wasn't to eat. It was for Easter." I leaned back in my seat, sniffling, and crossed my arms.

"Karina, you shouldn't have done that," Mom said, in a less reprimanding tone than I would have preferred.

Karina didn't get out of bed for the next two days except to use the bathroom, and aside from breastfeeding Owen, as he had been named, relied on my mother and me to care for the baby the rest of the time. We took turns burping him, changing his diaper, and rocking him while my sister slept. I was due to return to Vermont as school would be starting back up again, but I wished very badly to continue looking after Karina and Owen.

Karina planned to give legal custody of the baby to my Aunt Linette, Mom's youngest sister, who had been trying to get pregnant for years. Just twenty years old, Karina had given up her job at a health food store because of her declining health in the third trimester, and without child support from her ex-boyfriend—who knew nothing of Owen's existence anyhow—she had little hope of providing a good life for the baby.

My grandmother had brokered the deal. She and Linette persistently called Karina, each telling her how the best thing she could do for her son was to let him be raised by his loving great aunt and uncle. Linette promised Karina they would keep her involved in her son's life and that as soon as he was old enough to understand, they would tell him who his real mother was. Karina eventually consented.

As I headed to the airport to catch my return flight, I felt troubled about not getting to see baby Owen again. I was certain I had made things worse—and more confusing—for Karina by trying to talk her into keeping him. I'd promised that as soon as I graduated in three months' time, I would help her raise him. Of course, I had no idea of the magnitude of work that goes into raising a child; all I knew was that I loved my nephew and didn't want to lose him. I honestly believed that with my help, Karina would have had a good chance of establishing a home and a life for herself and her son. But there was no turning back; Linette and Paul would be flying out from Kansas in a matter of days to collect their new son.

After I returned to Vermont, Mom and Heidi kept me informed of the news back home. I received the first alarming call from my little sister, informing me that while I'd been on my way back to Vermont, Karina had started hemorrhaging. Only Heidi was home with her at the time, and she panicked when Karina fainted and collapsed on the bathroom floor. My little sister called 911, and an ambulance came to take them both to the hospital, where my mother and Winston soon joined them. Karina received a blood transfusion and remained in the hospital for twenty-four hours for observation. I was terrified to learn how bad a state she was in, from so far away where I couldn't do anything to help. I wished more than anything that I was still there to provide support.

I couldn't know how Karina felt in her heart, handing her baby off to our aunt and uncle, but it was apparent she didn't have the strength to care for him herself. It was weeks before she was back on her feet and ready to return to work. I fretted about both her physical and mental state throughout the ordeal. Devout Christians, Linette and Paul renamed the baby to Jacob, moving Owen to his middle name. Karina wasn't pleased about it but held her tongue.

Still fascinated by Native American traditions, Karina and Mom determined they should bury the placenta in the backyard as a symbolic gesture of some sort. My mother wrapped it in aluminum foil and stored it in the freezer to hold the burial ceremony once Karina had her strength back.

⌒

Mom tired of Winston, as she did of all her men eventually, and told him to stop coming around. I fought on his behalf and asked why she didn't want to marry him. In response, she kept repeating comments she'd made many, many times before about Winston being an old man and how she couldn't trust him.

Chapter 87

At the start of my senior year, a bulletin board went up in the high school building's main hallway displaying the college that each of the graduates planned to attend, a tradition designed to encourage and inspire other students.

In the previous year, I'd seen fine institutions such as Brown, Cornell, and U Penn listed. My peers weren't quite as ambitious, declaring schools closer to home. I, however, had no idea what to put on the board; I didn't even know how to go about applying to college. All I knew was that I couldn't count on either of my parents for help with the entrance process, financial aid applications, or so much as general encouragement, and it gave me anxiety to think about trying to secure higher education of any kind with such limited resources and support.

I didn't know where I should pick a school since I was about to be homeless upon graduation. The dichotomy of feeling like there were myriad options between the East Coast and returning to the West Coast, and yet no real options at all, was overwhelming.

When asked what I planned to do for a career, I would talk of becoming a psychologist. I found the field fascinating, especially given my complicated relationships with my parents. I had gotten an A in the psychology class I took at Satmardeva. However, when I heard of the stringent math requirements in the curriculum, the only subject in which I didn't excel, I talked myself out of exploring the field. I also had aspirations of becoming a chef, because it meant I would be creating—and, more importantly, tasting—delicious food for a profession. With Judy's help, I researched the Natural Gourmet Cookery School in New York, which seemed to be the only school that supported a vegetarian diet.

Then reality sunk in. Without knowing how to arrange housing or fend for myself in a state where I knew no one else, I planned to simply return to Washington, get a job, and decide what to do next after making some money. I missed my siblings, and I knew I could count on living with Karina. That was truly all I had going for me.

For the sake of having something to put on the board, I named the community college closest to where Mom was living. Each time I passed by the board I would look at it—just six student names, five with four-year institutions listed and mine with a two-year college. Satmardeva graduates didn't go to community college; they were primed to progress to universities, and many sought higher education after that. I felt ashamed of myself for setting my sights so low, but I felt overwhelmed whenever I contemplated applying for financial aid, filling out an application, and exploring a university campus on my own. What I had been able to accomplish with Satmardeva couldn't be repeated; certainly, no university in the world was going to have a school board that would hold my hand and advocate on my behalf to help me succeed.

As graduation day approached, Judy extended an offer for me to stay on at the school for an additional year to make up for having missed a good chunk of the fundamentals prior to arriving there. Some higher consciousness in my brain was moved by the school board's generosity and the fact that they truly cared about my education, but the ruling voice said that I had to return to Washington. I needed family around me again.

What Judy did convince me to do was tour the Natural Gourmet Cookery School in New York City en route to Washington. She offered to have the school's special fund pay for my return home if I agreed to the visit, and it warmed my heart yet again to have her looking out for me. Judy personally arranged all the details, which would have me traveling by bus to New York, where a Satmardeva alumna would escort me to the school, and I would then fly out from the John F. Kennedy Airport in Queens.

When graduation day came, no one in my immediate family attended. I'd always known there was no chance of it. It was financially impossible for any of them to afford a plane ticket, especially for a one-day affair. What did hurt, though, was neither parent expressing the sentiment of wishing to be present. Mom and Dad didn't demonstrate pride in our accomplishments any longer. Nothing had been done to celebrate Karina's graduation—which would have been all the more important for my parents to recognize since hers was the first graduation in our entire family—because Off-Campus High School didn't hold a commencement ceremony. The last time I could remember my parents having made a big deal about our academic achievements was when I was in the fifth grade.

One afternoon my parents had called Karina, Ben, and me into the kitchen.

"Have a seat," Mom said, her eyes dancing.

"What's going on?" Karina asked.

Both my parents had goofy grins on their faces.

"Just take a seat and close your eyes," Mom said playfully.

We did as we were told and sat down next to each other at the long dining table. I felt something alight on my head and heard the sound of a plate being set before me.

"Okay, open your eyes!" Mom said.

I gasped to discover a cake directly in front of me. With my mouth hanging open, I swiveled my head left and right and saw that my siblings each had a similar cake and we were all wearing gold paper crowns.

"You each got an A on your report card this semester!" Mom said, snapping a picture of us as we three sat in a row, beaming proudly. We attended Satmardeva together, where Ben was in the third grade, me in fifth, and Karina in eighth at the time.

"Is this all for me?" Ben asked, wrapping his hands protectively around his platter.

"Yes. You each get your own," Mom said.

"Well, dig in!" Dad said, handing out butter knives.

We eagerly started cutting out our own slices. Hidden beneath the chocolate frosting was a checkered cake—impossibly perfect brown and white alternating squares. I sucked in air. "How'd you make this?"

Again Karina, Ben, and I exchanged looks of delight.

"I bought a special kit to make a chocolate and vanilla cake," Mom said.

We had seen Mom produce many impressive cakes over the years, including the two-tiered beauty for her brother Dale's wedding, decorated with perfectly realistic pastel frosting flowers she piped around the edges. But this was a feat of magical proportions. We had never seen nor heard of such a thing as a checkered cake, and I felt thrilled to be recognized in this very special way.

Chapter 88

My classmates urged me to join them on the annual high school trip to Provincetown. Held in the summer just after graduation, it was a three-day opportunity to sleep in bunkhouses, eat in a communal kitchen, and swim in the ocean. I didn't want to ask the school to cover me yet again when they had already funded my participation in the event the previous year as well as my myriad trips back to the West Coast. No matter. I was going home! I would soon be with my siblings again. It was going to be a new chapter in our lives, a chance to right the wrongs.

I'd decided that the perfect way to celebrate a renewed bond with Mom was to present her with a mother's ring, the kind set with a birthstone for each of her children. I'd seen several women wearing such a ring, a lovely way to show maternal pride. What mother wouldn't want a sentimental reminder of her children?

I commissioned the ring from Malcolm, the same jeweler who had made my parents' wedding bands. The silver band would be set with lab-made gemstones: two amethysts, a ruby, a blue topaz, and lavender-colored alexandrite. I was able to afford the deposit of fifty dollars from my job at the health food store, but I had no idea how I was going to come up with the balance of $150 and have enough to ship my belongings home. Thus, when it came time to start packing my boxes, I had to ruthlessly pare down my already meager wardrobe. I donated the lot, including the Doc Marten boots that mom's gentlemen friends had given me for Christmas, to the school's fundraiser yard sale that they held every summer. At the eleventh hour, a generous graduation gift of $200 from Alyssa's parents enabled me pay off the ring and ship my boxes.

Chapter 89

On my bus trip down to New York City, I thought about all the people who had stepped forward to help me along the way in the absence of parental care so that I could reach graduation day, starting with my tenth-grade counselor Renee, to Judy and the rest of the staff at Satmardeva, to Alyssa's family, to those who hosted me in their homes during my time in Vermont. Whereas my own parents hadn't expressed concern about my well-being or future, people with no obligation to me whatsoever had helped me cross the divide from being in a hopeless situation to becoming a high school graduate.

When I disembarked at the Port Authority Bus Terminal in Times Square, I noticed my chaperone frowning as her gaze fell upon the large suitcase I was dragging alongside me on its rickety metal wheels. Rosemarie was a tall wisp of a twenty-something woman with flaxen hair pulled back in a low ponytail. She wore no makeup and was modestly dressed in black jeans and a forest-green top.

"Hi! I'm Angie!" I said, smiling at her.

"Yeah, hi, I'm Rosemarie," she said, still distractedly staring down at my suitcase. "I didn't know you would have luggage with you."

I wondered what the problem was.

Rosemarie grabbed hold of my suitcase and lurched toward the exit, appearing to be on the verge of toppling over. We stepped out onto the sidewalk and into the bright, chaotic world of Times Square. Larger-than-life moving billboards loomed overhead; acrid smoke billowed from food carts; and the din of horns, bicycle bells, talking, laughing, and shouting filled the air. My head swiveled frenetically as I took in all the activity.

My chaperone and I were immediately closed in on all sides by the throng of pedestrians darting past in both directions like schools of fish. Making excruciatingly slow progress, we attempted to move against the current toward the street, acutely aware we were in everyone's way. Rosemarie strained to get one arm high enough above the fray to hail a taxi. As she flailed her hand, the densely packed suitcase jerked along behind her, kicking out at a newspaper bin and a bus stop pole like a bucking bronco. We were blanketed by a suffocating humidity as we stood in the searing sun awaiting a ride.

Although I hadn't had to carry the suitcase—which the taxi driver took care of heaving into the trunk—I had still managed to break into a sweat. I was panting by the time I dove into the back seat. Relieved to find the cab air conditioned and to have survived the twenty-step expedition from the bus station to the car, I paused to consider the bizarre fact that this was my first taxi ride in my whole life.

Rosemarie instructed the driver to take us to the Flatiron district. I alternated between staring out the window at the myriad sights we passed along the way and politely smiling at my chaperone, who was devoid of expression.

"I had thought we would walk to the school," she said, "but with the luggage, a taxi was necessary."

I nodded, and nothing more was said.

"We're half a block from the address you gave me," the driver stated after a silent ride, "but I can't get any closer, due to the blockade. That'll be ten dollars."

A whole ten dollars? I thought. I couldn't believe it cost so much. Before I could dig out my limited pocket money, Rosemarie was already paying the man. I felt guilty about all the sacrifices she was having to make for a stranger. The driver pulled my suitcase from the trunk, and Rosemarie took ownership of it once again.

As we crossed the street, I stared at the police cars and ambulances that were blocking traffic. Just outside the entry to the school, a man lay sprawled on the pavement next to his mangled bicycle. Though wearing a helmet, he was either unconscious or dead.

"Will he be okay?" I asked no one in particular, as I stared in horror. *What a dangerous city this is,* I thought.

Rosemarie's gait didn't slow; she had momentum on her side and wasn't about to stop. She barged ahead into the school's entry, and I ran to catch up. Entering the reception area, my chaperone thrust the suitcase to the side of the check-in desk, informed the receptionist of my appointment, and asked the woman to call a taxi to the airport for me once my tour concluded.

"Thank you so much for all your help, Rosemarie," I said.

"You're welcome," she called, already heading for the door. "Good luck." She disappeared back into the chaos of the city, to return to work.

I thoroughly enjoyed my tour of the school, where I got to watch students in action making pastries. The rest of the world fell away as I stood within that enormous kitchen, beholding everyone in their professional chef wear. They each had such focus, demonstrating a clear desire to master the art of cooking.

The program truly appealed to me, but for the fact I hadn't the first clue about how to establish housing and fend for myself in the city. The support structure I'd had in Vermont didn't exist in New York; there wasn't a Judy here to help me investigate options and plan a course of action. Plus, with all I had witnessed in the short span of time between Times Square and arriving at the school, it was clear I had no place in that world.

Thus concluded my sole college visit, with me deciding it just wasn't something I could pull off on my own. My parents didn't have degrees, and Karina hadn't attended college after discovering that Uncle Sam didn't cover the cost of higher education for military personnel in the reserves. We were a working-class family, and I couldn't envision pulling off anything more than a job at a health food store and living paycheck to paycheck, as I was familiar with seeing at home.

Once the tour wrapped up, the secretary ushered me to a cab waiting at the curb. In my last conversation with her, Mom had told me she was looking forward to me coming home and to having all her children in the same state. I couldn't wait to see her face when I presented her with the ring I'd commissioned for her. I boarded the plane with a heart full of hope.

On my flight to Washington, I indulged myself with the fantasy of deplaning to see Mom and Dad standing there smiling, their arms wrapped around each other's backs. They would be flanked by my brothers and sisters. I would proudly show off my diploma, and then we'd all head home, giddy about being reunited.

However, I arrived to find only Mom, Karina, and Ryan waiting at the gate. My eyes were drawn to my little brother's feet, on which he was wearing an older sibling's flip flops that were several sizes too large. It had likely taken some pleading and cajoling on my mother's part to get him to accompany them to the airport.

There was no fanfare for my return. Heidi was away at a summer camp, for which she'd earned a full scholarship, and Ben was still living with Dad and Maude an hour and a half north of Mom. My father probably wasn't even aware I was back on the West Coast.

Mom and Karina promptly launched into a description about all the challenges at home. The barrage of negativity didn't stop as we collected my luggage, got into the car, and drove south to the duplex. They talked about how temperamental Heidi was now that she was a teenager, about my father being a deadbeat dad, and about the struggles of living paycheck to paycheck. I kept quiet and turned my gaze to the dreary, overcast sky, which mirrored my rising dread. I feared returning had been a big mistake.

Nevertheless, as planned, I handed Mom the mother's ring inside a small white jewelry box once we reached her duplex. I felt proud to be able to give her such a lavish gift.

"It's beautiful, sweetheart," she said, slipping it on. "Thank you." Her genuine smile all but confirmed that things were going to be different this time around.

Chapter 90

Soon after, Mom returned to living with Winston, while Karina and I secured our own apartment nearby in the outskirts of Tacoma. The best we could afford was a basic one-bedroom unit with a brown shag carpet and beige kitchen appliances in an old two-story complex. I had been hired at minimum wage in a deli located within the same health food store where my sister worked the stockroom and Mom was a floor manager.

I often wanted to drive up to Winston's house for dinner to be surrounded by family, but Karina couldn't be convinced to accompany me. She never talked about it, but I knew she still felt unwelcome there ever since she had stolen from Winston. Sometimes I'd just go by myself, but at other times I felt guilty about leaving my sister alone and would remain at the apartment.

As we headed into winter, we only kept the heat on in our bedroom as we couldn't afford an increase in the electricity bill. We had to dress in layers and brace for the cold each time we needed to use the bathroom or make a cup of tea. We were back to sharing a bed, this time just a mattress on the floor, which helped us keep warm at night.

Chapter 91

Karina and I learned of a woman originally from our hometown community who held Sunday services out of her house just a half hour's drive away. I was thrilled to finally have a spiritual connection in Washington, and we started attending her service every weekend. Although we now sat on the floor of a small cabin instead of the long worship hall in Vermont, the effect was the same.

Eloise was a sweet, humble woman with silver hair and a gentle, calming demeanor. I was grateful for the opportunity to worship with other devotees again, while simultaneously feeling betrayed that my parents hadn't bothered finding out that Eloise offered an outlet for us to have some semblance of a community in Washington, albeit with just a handful of other devotees who traveled from great distances. It would've meant an hour-and-a-half drive each way from where we used to live as a family, but religion was never about convenience.

When the used car Karina and I had purchased from a neighbor broke down and would cost more to repair than the car was worth, Winston kindly offered to let us borrow the decade-old navy-blue Thunderbird sitting unused in his garage. It was an ugly thing but in perfect driving condition, and we certainly appreciated the free transportation.

Although Mom had given up her duplex to move back in with Winston, the next thing I knew, she was breaking up with him for good. Everything had seemed picture-perfect to me in that charming little house of his.

"He's just a doddering old man," Mom said. "He's always trying to push a limp one on me. He's a liar too. I don't trust anything he says."

If I were to say anything in his defense, I knew she would list all the occasions on which she was certain he hadn't been straight with her. My heart fell upon realizing that Winston wasn't destined to become my stepfather as I'd hoped. Instead, his name was joining the growing list of temporary father figures who sooner or later exited our lives forever.

Since she now needed a place to live, Mom begged Karina to break our lease and move into an apartment with her in a brand-new complex. It was the last thing in the world I wanted to do since I didn't trust Mom, but Karina felt we couldn't turn her down because Mom was going to be out on the street otherwise. We relented and agreed to all go in on a spacious three-bedroom apartment, which, incidentally, turned out to be the nicest place we'd ever lived.

I laid down some ground rules for my mother first: she wasn't allowed to have any men over, and we would all three be considered equals since we were splitting the rent in thirds. She heartily agreed, and we made the recently constructed Belmont apartment complex in Tacoma our new home.

In addition to Heidi and Ryan, Mom brought her cat, Zima, which she'd adopted while living at Winston's house. Ben moved in with us as well, and for the first time in years, all five children lived together under one roof.

When I noticed that Mom had hung the still-life painting of the ceramic jug and apples in the dining room, I smiled at it. *Maybe this time we really have a shot at rekindling our family bond,* I thought.

For a couple of months, it was actually a dream come true: we were living in the closest approximation of harmony I'd seen in a long time, even though we didn't get back into the habit of taking meals together every evening as I would have preferred. Everyone was on different schedules, the three youngest were often away at friends' houses, and Karina started dating a man who was a customer at the health food store where we worked.

Karina and Ben shared a room with bunk beds, Heidi and I shared a full-size bed in our room, and Mom took the primary bedroom. Ryan slept in a nest he'd created on her floor using several blankets and a pillow. He had decided he didn't want to go to school anymore, and some days it was impossible to rouse him from his nest on Mom's bedroom floor. The rest of us would go to our respective jobs and schools, and Mom would give up after all the ineffectual scolding and just leave him there. Other days she would keep after him, saying, "You need to get up, Ryan," in her most stern tone. Unimpressed, my brother took his time rising and getting ready. It had never occurred to me at the age of eleven to protest school.

Mom complained bitterly to Karina and me about how much trouble Ryan was and how she wished she could send him to live with Winston. Her irrational logic bothered me given that she had broken up with Winston. Just because he had been good to my little brother when they'd all lived together didn't mean he wanted to inherit her problems, especially when Winston and Mom weren't in a relationship anymore.

Winston seemed heartbroken, and we missed him, so Karina invited him to meet us at the espresso stand where she worked the early morning shift on weekends for extra income. It was located right outside a ferry terminal where the ferries mostly shuttled prison workers out to McNeil Island and back. Occasionally prisoners were transported to and from the ferry by special unmarked buses. The passengers were identifiable by their beige jumpsuits and matching Converse sneakers. I thought it was an especially cool uniform.

It was peaceful and quiet down by the water, and I enjoyed hanging out while Karina worked, especially because I'd get a free latte out of it. Customers came in waves according to the ferry schedule, so there was a lot of downtime in between.

Winston spent about an hour there with us, catching up on our lives. It was sad how much he clearly loved our mother and wished to get her back. He had become a counselor at a halfway house. I was proud of him for leaving the prison and using his efforts to help those who sought to get their lives back on track.

When the visit reached its natural conclusion, I looked him in the eye. "I still love you, Winston," I said. The qualifier—"even though you and Mom aren't together anymore"—was left unspoken.

"You know I'll always care about you kids," he said. He cleared his throat and looked away. He didn't meet our eyes as he gave us each a hug before leaving.

My sister and I foolishly thought we could beg on Winston's behalf for Mom to give him another chance. But she was furious with us when we told her about the visit.

"How dare you see him without asking my permission!"

"But Mom," I said, "we miss him."

"I don't care. You still should have asked. I don't want you seeing him anymore."

Karina rolled her eyes. I wanted to yell at Mom for bringing Winston into our lives, forcing us to make nice, and then expecting us to instantly cut him off the moment she did, but I bit my tongue. It was obvious she had no sentimentality to appeal to. Whenever Mom fancied a man, we were forced to hear about his many great qualities. Once the magic wore off came the descriptions of his many more negative attributes.

Chapter 92

I started rollerblading at night in a well-lit parking lot with a new friend I had made, and though I would enter the apartment quietly and not turn on any lights when I returned at ten o'clock, Mom complained in the morning about having her sleep disrupted.

"I don't want you staying out past bedtime," she demanded. "I need my sleep."

Though I was angered by her pulling rank like that when I was her equal as far as the rental contract was concerned, I didn't argue as I knew it was pointless.

Before long, Mom broke the cardinal rule and started having men over. More specifically, it was one man whom none of us liked. Leroy would arrive in a blue jumpsuit with a name patch stitched onto the chest and leave his leather work boots by the door. He was the kind of guy who, even with two sticks of gum in hand, wouldn't think to offer one to a child in his company. If he acknowledged us at all, it was only a nod in our direction. He and Mom would immediately disappear into her bedroom.

I harbored a smoldering resentment just below the surface of my calm exterior. The injustice of having my space, an apartment that I paid exactly one third of the rent for, violated by an unwelcome stranger was too much to bear. Leroy was, in my opinion, the worst of the visitors my mother had entertained over the years. It was disappointing to realize that she hadn't changed a bit. This wasn't the picture of the ideal family life I'd had in my head when we all moved into the apartment together.

Mom's relationship with this unfriendly man was made even more intolerable when she informed Karina and me that she had met him at a dance club, a venue where she'd found she was the only White woman present. According to her, all the women in the room gave her the stink eye as she made her rounds and danced with several men. At one point she left her drink unattended at the bar. Leroy was the last man she met that night, and they went to his apartment afterward. In the morning, they both professed to each other that they weren't the type to have a one-night stand. Leroy further told her he was not in the habit of going to dance clubs, but on that occasion, his friends had coerced him into joining them.

Mom told me she was certain one of those resentful women had slipped Spanish fly into her drink.

"What's Spanish fly?" I asked, picturing a red bug circling over my mother's cocktail.

"You know—that drug that removes your inhibitions," Mom said.

I didn't for one second believe she needed anything as elaborate as roofies to convince her to fall into a stranger's bed. What would the spiteful ladies have gained by drugging her? If anything, it would make more sense for Leroy himself to have been guilty of foul play.

After Leroy left our apartment one evening, I stood in front of Mom and demanded that this behavior stop per our agreement before taking the apartment together.

"I am your mother," she sternly reminded me, "and you need to show me the proper respect."

Having been duped into living with Mom again but not having any other options available to me, I didn't push the issue. She couldn't be reasoned with, and I was tired of being disrespected, especially now that I was an adult and financially contributing to keeping her off the street. Though I no longer knew what "normal" was, I knew what didn't feel right.

I was reminded of an old fable about a scorpion coercing a frog to give her a ride on his back across a lake. In the story, Frog expresses his wariness at being stung.

"Now, why would I do a thing like that?" Scorpion said. "Then we would both surely die."

Thus, Frog agreed to carry Scorpion across the lake, and just as they passed the midpoint, Scorpion stung Frog.

"Why did you do that?" Frog asked. "Now we'll both drown."

"It's my nature," said Scorpion, and indeed, they both perished.

Mom likewise made decisions as though there were no consequences, the recklessness of which not only angered me but also increased my anxiety about how the inevitable consequences would impact whoever was caught in her wake. I was yet again going down with the ship and needed to get off once and for all. It was clear now more than ever that I had to limit my exposure to my mother to avoid getting stung.

Little by little our family's code had been chipped away until it felt like our whole world had turned upside down. It started with the cross-country move, then no longer attending Sunday services, followed by the divorce, the carousing, the child neglect, and then previously prohibited foods and vices becoming acceptable. I was done standing quietly on the sidelines and resolved to no longer permit my exposure to an ever-escalating string of lifestyle changes so far off track from where we'd started as a family.

Chapter 93

One evening, I noticed Heidi's backpack on my bedroom floor. It was unzipped, revealing the unexpected presence of dozens of individually wrapped syringes with hypodermic needles bunched together in a clear plastic bag. I pulled the bag out in alarm to find that sitting just underneath it was a strange glass pipe, which I assumed was for smoking marijuana, as I'd never seen drug paraphernalia before. It was as if she'd wanted me to find the contraband. I immediately brought the discovery to my mother's attention and demanded to know what she was going to do about it. Lying on her bed reading, she stopped to laugh at my dramatic delivery.

"Oh, Angie," she said, "I'm sure it's nothing."

I sighed in exasperation and went to Karina's bedroom, where I found her also lying on her bed reading.

"I can't believe Mom isn't worried that Heidi might be doing drugs," I exclaimed, with my hands propped on my hips.

"Uh, newsflash," Karina said, momentarily ceasing to chew her fingernails, "that's because Mom smokes pot." She returned to biting her nails.

It was clearly old news. Apparently, smoking pot was one of two activities Mom was regularly engaging in with Leroy behind closed doors. I guess I was the only one with my head buried in the sand or the only one sensitive enough to be disturbed by this information at any rate.

Then I recalled an odd statement my mother had made three years prior when I asked her whether she thought anything about her lifestyle was inappropriate. Referring to the neglect and unwelcome visitors we kids had to suffer in our apartment, I had hoped to read at least a glimmer of remorse on her face.

"No," she said, frowning at me. "I have nothing to hide. In fact, if you were to go through my drawers and find drugs or anything else you didn't like, I wouldn't care. I'm an adult and can do whatever I want."

I was so put off by her rebellious attitude that I didn't even consider whether there might actually be drugs stashed in her sock drawer. Anyone else in my place would have been prompted to rifle through her drawers immediately to find out what on earth she was referring to. It all added up now; she must have been smoking pot since way back then. And she must have assumed at the time that my question was fueled by finding her stash.

Even though it was after ten o'clock at night, I rang up Vanessa's house where my sister was staying the night. When Heidi got on the phone, I told her about finding the paraphernalia in her backpack and proceeded to interrogate her about it. She laughed it off.

"I have a diabetic friend at school who asked me to hold on to her insulin needles," she said. I didn't know what insulin needles looked like, so I couldn't argue that point any further.

"And what about the pipe?" I demanded.

She claimed that the pipe, likewise, was being held for a friend. It felt frustrating to know that my thirteen-year-old sister wasn't being straight with me, but there was nothing more I could do. It was also distressing that no one else was concerned about her behavior. "I heard from Mom that your school counselor tried calling her at work today," I continued, in a softer tone. "What was the phone call for?"

Heidi told me that she had broken down crying in class and didn't know what had triggered it. She felt embarrassed, and the teacher sent her to the counselor's office, where she confessed that she had been feeling suicidal. I told her I understood how she felt and made her promise she would take good care of herself.

"I love you, Ang," she said.

"I love you too, Heidi," I said, before hanging up.

After that, she started spending weeks on end living at her friend's house. When Mom called her to ask when she was coming home, Heidi made the mistake of informing her that Vanessa's mother was more of a parent to her. I didn't hear the end of it for days.

"How dare Heidi say that to me," she kept exclaiming to Karina and me. "I'm sure Vanessa's mother is just some trashy woman. I've heard all she does is sit around watching TV, and she's a smoker. What's she got that's so special? The nerve of that kid!"

⁓

One afternoon I took a phone call at the apartment meant for my mother, who was at work. I asked if there was a message I could relay to her.

"This is Peter Robinson, head of Macy's security at the Tacoma Mall," said the serious voice on the other end of the line. "We have a Heidi Kiehne here in custody."

My voice caught in my throat, so he went on.

"Heidi and her friend Vanessa were witnessed stealing merchandise. Normally we would turn these situations over to the police, but given that the girls are minors, we're going to release them with a warning. They are forbidden from entering any Macy's location for a year. We've already contacted Vanessa's mother to collect her. Is someone in your family able to retrieve Heidi?"

"Yes," I said. "I am her older sister, and I will take responsibility for her."

I drove to the mall, fuming. My mind was filled with images of Heidi turning to a life of crime. This event could signal the start of a downward spiral. There was a trend in the Tacoma region of teens selling out any opportunity for future success by getting pregnant in high school and dropping out or getting into drugs and drinking. I couldn't accept this fate for my little sister.

As I pulled up outside the rear entrance of the Macy's store, where Peter had told me to go, I saw Heidi trudging, head down, toward my car. I was surprised that they didn't make me come inside for an official hand-off.

"*Are you crazy?*" I shouted as soon as Heidi was in the passenger seat.

She looked away, ashamed.

"What the hell were you thinking?" I demanded, as I started heading back home. "You could've been arrested! You could've been sent to juvy! You know all the teenagers in this hellhole end up getting sent there. Your life is over if you go there! You need to turn your life around, Heidi. Don't go down this path."

"I'm sorry, Ang—" she started to say softly.

"'Sorry' isn't going to keep you out of juvy," I said curtly, cutting her off. "Look, your parents might not be there to give you any guidance, but I'm certainly not going to stand by and watch you throw your life away. You need to get your act together. As far as I'm concerned, you're grounded."

Chapter 94

At the age of eighteen, I attempted to call a truce with Dad. Without telling anyone else in the family of my plan, I asked him to meet me at Bite of India, our family's favorite restaurant at Crossroads Mall in our old stomping grounds on the east side of Bellevue. A great deal of time had gone by since we'd last spoken, so I thought the familiar territory would put us both at ease. It necessitated an hour-and-a-half drive drive north for me, coming from Tacoma, the longest road trip I had undertaken by myself.

All the way up I rehearsed what I would say. I arrived at the food court early in order to compose myself before Dad arrived. Settling at a table at the outskirts, hoping it would afford us more privacy, I ordered vegetable biryani out of habit. My meal was served on a red plastic tray, the same as when I'd first visited the mall four years prior. I found I could do little more than push the rice around my plate with a fork. My stomach was churning. The knots tightened as soon as I saw my father making his way across the food court.

"Hi," he said flatly, his face drawn. He didn't remove his coat or driving cap after taking a seat across from me at the square plastic table.

"Would you like to order anything?" I asked, trying not to let my voice waver.

"No thanks," he said, as if I'd just asked him to purchase a magazine subscription.

"Your children miss you and would like to see you," I said, kicking off my rehearsed speech.

"You kids don't want me for a father anymore," he said. He didn't sound sad; his tone was a mixture of anger and resignation.

"No one ever said that." I spoke slowly, choosing my words carefully as I went on to explain that Dad shouldn't take our behavior personally. My siblings and I had merely reacted, as children do, to their parents splitting up. His raised eyebrow surprised me, especially given that he worked with children for a living. His skepticism indicated complete disregard, as though this was a new theory and not a known phenomenon backed by modern psychology and likely thousands of case studies. "It's not true that we don't want you for our father," I pressed. "We want you in our lives."

"You kids only want me when it's time for me to open my wallet," Dad said, looking off to the side and drumming his fingers on the table.

His eyebrows were pinched together, wrinkling his forehead. This time it wasn't to make himself appear aloof—he was in fact done with me. Done with being a father. What hurt more than words was the disinterest I saw in his eyes.

Yet I continued trying to make a case for my siblings and me. Though I wasn't there with their knowledge, I felt it was important that someone try to bridge the divide. After all, there was one evening that Heidi had come to me with a concerned look on her face to tell me Ben was crying on his bed. When I asked her why, she shrugged. "He won't say, but I know it's about Dad."

I went into my brother's room and found him facedown on his bed, sobbing. I sat at the edge and rubbed his back, encouraging him to talk about it. "Why doesn't Dad care about me?" he asked between chest-heaves.

"Oh Ben ...," I said, grasping for an answer. "Dad loves you. He does. He just doesn't know how to show it right now."

How had things come to this? How had the father who had raised me, whom I had adored and been nearly inseparable from for twelve whole years, become this coldhearted? I could still remember what it felt like to be carried in his strong arms from the car to the house when, as a small child, I fell asleep in the back seat on a trip home. Vaguely aware of the transition, I relished the comfort of being scooped up and carried gently to bed.

Everything was backward. Dad should have been asking for my forgiveness for abandoning his children, for getting remarried without telling us, and for giving away my pet rat. And yet there I was, shamefully groveling for his love.

"Well," he said, standing up. "It looks like we've reached an impasse." With that, he walked off.

I stared at my father's back in disbelief, tears streaming silently down my cheeks. Wiping them away quickly with a napkin, I didn't want to be seen crying at a plastic table in a food court.

The effort it took to pull myself up out of the chair felt as laborious as fighting against an ocean current. The sensation continued as I bussed my table and headed outside to the old Thunderbird that Winston was still loaning me even though Mom wasn't with him anymore.

My investment of a three-hour round-trip drive and all but prostrating myself before my father hadn't paid off. I'd been given less than thirty minutes to plead my case. Sickened to the pit of my stomach, I started the drive back down south.

Dad would have immediately returned to his house, to Maude's side. Would he tell her what had transpired? Would they, together, scoff in disbelief? And what then—would they go out for an afternoon of fun activities, carrying on with their child-free lives?

I reviewed in my mind all the ugly interactions that had transpired between us over the past few years since my parents split up and still couldn't believe things had come to this. How could Dad's heart have hardened to the point where seeing my forlorn face didn't stir up any emotions?

Tears kept me company the length of the drive home, and I dabbed at my eyes repeatedly with the sleeve of my sweatshirt, trying not to let my vision become dangerously blurred. I found myself hoping, yearning, that for once my mother would be home, available, and receptive to providing the emotional support I so badly needed. To my surprise and relief, I found her lying on her bed reading *The Celestine Prophecy*. I collapsed next to her. Tears streamed down my face as I relayed the events of the afternoon. She stroked my back comfortingly.

"I'm sorry, Ang, that you didn't get what you'd hoped out of it," Mom said softly. It felt reassuring to have her behave in such a motherly fashion. "He's emotionally unavailable," she continued. "That's why I left him."

Chapter 95

I felt increasingly unfulfilled and frustrated about the state of things at home. Having been duped into becoming my mother's roommate, I was routinely disrespected and saw no future for myself in dead-end Tacoma. I didn't want to live with her anymore. Joining the Peace Corps was something I longed to do, but unfortunately my application wouldn't even be entertained since I didn't have a bachelor's degree.

Miraculously, a one-way ticket back to the East Coast was presented in the form of a phone call from my old employer at the health food store where I'd worked part-time as a senior in high school.

"Hello, Angie," Miriam said, in her sweet, low voice. "I'm looking to hire the store's first full-time salesclerk. I immediately thought of you and wondered if you might be interested."

"Oh, I'm interested!" I said, grinning.

"Of course, I understand that you'll need some time to consider," she continued.

"Nope, I'm in!" I said. "I'll absolutely take it. You have no idea how perfect your timing is."

Miriam told me that the position was forty hours a week and that she knew of a room I could rent in a house near the store. The cherry on top was that she'd come into possession of a donut-baking machine just like my father used to use before switching to a more economical deep fryer. I smiled at the thought of serving our spiritual community just like Dad used to. I was going back to Vermont!

I'd be sad to leave my siblings again, but the comfort of living with them didn't outweigh the misery of living with Mom. And it was overwhelming dealing with Ryan and Heidi's rebelliousness on top of Mom's. Living together again as a family hadn't turned out to be as fulfilling as I'd anticipated.

I wasn't looking forward to breaking the news to Mom when she returned home from work that evening.

"What about our leasing agreement?" she asked when I told her. "You're going to be leaving me without a third of the rent money."

"You violated that agreement first," I said, looking her square in the eye, "by bringing men home."

We stared at each other for a moment, and I could tell by the way her shoulders slumped ever so slightly that she knew full well she had no leverage.

"I can't live here anymore," I said. "I'm unhappy."

"Well, do whatever you need to do," she said, frowning.

The fact that she didn't demonstrate concern for the consequences of her actions freed me from the guilt of breaking my commitment with the lease. After what had transpired with my father at the food court and getting burned by my mother, I resolved not to count on them for anything ever again.

I put in my two weeks' notice at work and packed up my clothes. Given that I had so little money and planned to stop in Philadelphia en route to my destination, I bought a Greyhound bus ticket rather than taking a flight. This way I could meet my pen pal, Kai, in person and tell him I was in love with him.

The day I left, Mom followed me down to Karina's car. She stopped near the bumper, and we hugged briefly.

"I won't be back," I said as I opened the passenger door.

"Okay," she said matter-of-factly. "I hope you find what you're looking for."

I slid inside and closed the door. I wondered whether my mother would remain where she stood, waving with tears in her eyes as Grandma used to after our family visits to North Carolina. Glancing in the side mirror, I saw that Mom was already gone. There were no wet eyes that day.

After Karina hugged me and wished me well, I stood at the edge of the Greyhound platform in downtown Tacoma, feeling completely alone in the world. I wore a faded green hoodie, a white T-shirt imprinted with a vitamin brand, and jeans. Staring down at my Converse sneakers, I thought about all the circumstances that had led me there, on the verge of this journey.

"It can't be that bad, can it?" I heard a voice say.

I lifted my eyes to see a fresh-faced young man who couldn't have been more than ten years my senior, snuggling a toddler in his arms. I stared at him.

"It can't be that bad, can it?" he repeated, smiling exaggeratedly as though to indicate that I too should smile.

You have no idea, I thought. For a split second I considered telling him my life story. I imagined watching his face morph through the emotions that someone who had never experienced such travesties would feel while listening to the barrage of sordid details that had characterized my teenage years. But it would embarrass him, and I didn't want his child to hear such inappropriate things, so I simply smiled back.

The lonely, impersonal view out the window as the bus passed industrial buildings and smokestacks starkly illustrated my thoughts. My departure hadn't sent up any red flags for my parents. Despite the neglect I had experienced since their separation four years prior and the fact that I was no longer a minor, it still struck me as odd that they couldn't be bothered to worry about their teenage daughter embarking on a three-day journey across the country by bus.

Retaining a window seat for the journey gave me something to lean against as I slept with an arm slung protectively over my backpack in the seat next to me. I kept the hood of my sweatshirt up, hoping the antisocial look would dissuade other passengers from interacting with me or, worse, messing with my stuff while I was sleeping. There was nothing to do for three days but stare out the window, listen to music on my Walkman, and eat fast food at rest stops along the way.

Despite being exhausted and disheveled, I felt increasingly giddy as the bus drew closer to Philadelphia. More than anything in the whole world, I yearned to feel like I belonged somewhere, like I'd found my home. I was betting everything I had on finding it with a pen pal I was about to meet in person for the first time.

Acknowledgments

Thank you to my editor Amy Ashby and publisher, Warren Publishing, for believing in my work and making my debut book a reality, as well as Melissa Long and Melisa Graham for supporting and improving upon my vision.

Thank you to my younger sister for providing valuable editing services and corroborating shared memories.

Thank you to Dr. Nadia Lemp-Nguyen for helping me work through my grief, find my voice, and live my truth.

Thank you to Jon Reiner, author and outstanding teacher on the craft of memoir writing.

Thank you to Phil Cohen for being an enthusiastic, insightful developmental editor through the lens of a Hollywood insider.

Special thanks to Barbara Villasenor for reviewing my first five chapters and providing insights on current publishing trends.

Finally, a big thanks to my early readers for providing support and feedback.

www.ingramcontent.com/pod-product-compliance
Lightning Source LLC
Chambersburg PA
CBHW021356090426
42742CB00009B/880